Living with a
Bichon Frisé

Edited by Roger Dunger

BARRON'S

THE QUESTION OF GENDER
The "he" pronoun is used throughout this book in favor of the rather impersonal "it," but no gender bias is intended.

ACKNOWLEDGEMENTS
Action Shots Photography (www.actionshots.me.uk) for the image on page 69; Alan V. Walker for the image on page 81; Lisa T. Silhan, Paw Prints Professional Pet Photography for the image on page 91; Marc Henrie for the images on pages 1, 8, 94, and 96; Victor Steel Photography for the image on page 90.

First edition for the United States and Canada published in 2005 by Barron's Educational Series, Inc.

First published in Great Britain in 2005 by Ringpress Books

All inquiries should be addressed to:
Barron's Educational Series, Inc.
250 Wireless Boulevard
Hauppauge, NY 11788
http://www.barronseduc.com

International Standard Book Number 0-7641-5775-2
Library of Congress Catalog Card Number 2003115645

PRINTED IN CHINA THROUGH PRINTWORKS INT. LTD.
9 8 7 6 5 4 3 2 1

CONTENTS

and cleaning; Scissoring; Finishing touches); Family life; Adolescent needs (Neutering pros and cons); Veteran care; Euthanasia.

CHAPTER ONE

INTRODUCING THE BICHON FRISÉ

With his cute, teddy bear looks and whiter-than-white coat, the Bichon Frisé is a true star of the dog world. But there is a great deal more to this little dog than his glamorous good looks.

Small he may be, but the Bichon has a larger-than-life personality. This may explain why he features in the Non-Sporting category in the American Kennel Club, rather than in the Toy group. He may have been bred purely as a companion dog, but he is not a pet that simply enjoys being mollycoddled—he likes getting stuck into all the activities and pursuits that larger dogs do... and more!

MADE IN THE MED

Small white dogs are believed to have existed in the Mediterranean area from 600 B.C. The Bichon Frisé descends from the Barbet, or Water Spaniel, which became known as the Barbichon (from the French *barbiche*, meaning "beard"),

shortened to Bichon. Four breeds came from this Bichon family:

- Bichon Maltais (Maltese)
- Bichon Bolognais (Bolognese)
- Bichon Havanais (Havanase)
- Bichon Teneriffe (later the Bichon Frisé)

The Mediterranean was a significant trading area, and sailors arriving in the region were eager to buy and sell. Bichon dogs were frequently used to barter with, and they were taken all over the world, ensuring that each type developed independently.

The Bichon we are interested in, the Bichon Frisé, landed in the Canary Islands off the west coast of Africa, where he took his name from the largest island, Teneriffe. He traveled elsewhere with Spanish sailors too, but maintained his exotic name, adding to his desirability as a somewhat decadent, unusual companion.

BIRD DOG!

The Canary Islands actually have nothing to do with canaries! The name comes from canaria, which is Latin for "dog."

EUROPEAN UNION

It is thought that the Bichon was rediscovered by Italian sailors in the 14th century, who re-introduced the dogs to Europe, where they were particularly popular with royalty and nobility in Italy, and later in France and Spain. In addition to being first-rate companions, they also acted as good watchdogs, something modern Bichon breeds still excel at.

The Bichon Teneriffe was introduced as a royal court dog in France during the reign of Francis I, at the beginning of the 16th century. But its popularity soared towards the end of the century, during Henry III's rule. The king was said to be so enchanted by the breed that he carried the little white dogs about in a basket tied with ribbons around his neck.

Throughout history, royalty has dictated fashions, and it wasn't long before ladies of the court were seen carrying the Teneriffe dogs in baskets or shawls. Interestingly, it is thought that the French verb *bichonner*, meaning "to pamper and to beautify," originated from their love affair with the breed.

Previously used for bartering by sailors, the dogs were now given as diplomatic gifts between royal courts, and their popularity spread to the nobility too.

But the French Revolution of 1789 took its toll on the breed. Associated with the decadent old order, the Bichon Teneriffe lost popularity when the aristocracy and royalty were overthrown. It enjoyed a brief resurgence in Napoleon III's era (1852–1870), but then fell from grace. After centuries of being popular playthings of the nobility, the Bichon was out of favor.

The Bichon was a favorite with the royal families of Europe.

Pioneers realized the importance of keeping the breed pure.

CANINE MUSE

Beautiful to look at, with his wonderful coat and large, lustrous eyes, the Bichon Frisé is a work of art—in fact, he has inspired many great painters. Spanish artist Goya (1746–1828) painted white dogs in a number of his works, including a Bichon type in his 1795 work *The Duchess of Alba*. This painting shows the dog in a "lion" trim, where the coat from the dog's last rib to the hocks has been trimmed, and the rest left natural. This coat style was popular on the Continent, and several breeds sported it; indeed, it remains a recognized Poodle clip, and is now most associated with the Lowchen.

British artist Joshua Reynolds (1723–1792) also featured Bichons in his paintings *Miss Nellie O'Brien* (c1760) being the most famous example. In *The Love Letter* (c1770) by French artist Jean-Honoré Fragonard (1732–1806), another white dog is depicted that is similar to today's Bichon.

STREET DOGS

Fortunately, this was not the end of our plucky little dog. The end of the 18th century saw the Bichon Teneriffe scavenging the streets and befriending a new class of admirer. He accompanied organ grinders and beggars, and even turned up in circuses, earning his living by doing tricks—leaping, walking on his hind legs and pawing the air. Living on his wits, the Bichon ensured his own survival.

VIVE LA FRANCE!

Until after the First World War (1914–1918), Bichon Teneriffes took care of themselves, but there was no concerted effort to keep the breed type pure. However, soldiers returning from postings in the war brought home the pretty little white dogs they found in various European countries, and French and Belgian breeders soon took the Bichon under their wings, breeding with the limited stock

The first Breed Standard was drawn up in 1933.

Am. Ch. Sasikay Wolmara Lady Of Spain.
Official recognition for the Bichon in the United States came in 1973.

that was available to safeguard the dog's future.

In March 1933, the first Breed Standard was devised, written by Madame Bouctovangniez, the president of the French Toy Club. By now, the Bichon Teneriffe was popularly called the Bichon à Poil Frisé, meaning "the Bichon of the curly hair." When it came to deciding on an official, permanent name for the breed, there was a great deal of debate and little consensus. Exasperated by the lack of progress, the head of the Breed Standards Committee for the Fédération Cynologique Internationale (FCI,

the canine governing body for Continental Europe), Madame Nizet de Leemans, simply asked what the breed looked like. The reply was that it looked like a fluffy little dog, and so the breed was called just that—Bichon Frisé—and the name has stuck.

The following year, in 1934, the Bichon Frisé was entered into the French Kennel Club stud book, the final step to becoming an official, established breed.

CROSSING THE ATLANTIC

The first record of a purebred Bichon in the

United States was in 1956, when Helene and Francis Picault of Dieppe, France, migrated to Milwaukee, Wisconsin, accompanied by numerous Bichons Frisés (initially seven, with the addition of two more a few months later).

Eager to establish the breed in their adopted country, the Picaults faced a difficult task. Without kennel club recognition, there was not the interest in the breed that they had hoped for. Nevertheless, a firm fan base was slowly established. The breed caught the eye of Azalea Gascoigne, a Milwaukee Dachshund breeder, and later, when the Picault family moved to San Diego, California, a Collie breeder called Gertrude Fournier also became a convert.

In 1964 the Bichon Frisé Club of America was founded. Azalea Gascoigne was appointed the first president, and Gertrude Fournier the secretary. Through the club's hard work in promoting the breed, interest in the Bichon grew, but official American Kennel Club recognition was not forthcoming.

Thanks to something of an image makeover, that was soon to change. At a breed club meeting in 1969, Frank Sabella, a Poodle expert, gave a grooming demonstration on how to wash, dry and scissor a Bichon. This did wonders for how the breed was presented—and received—and the Bichon Frisé was finally accepted into the Miscellaneous Class in 1971, listed in the stud book in 1972, and given full recognition in 1973.

BRITISH FANS

Given the closer proximity of Britain to France, you would have thought that the Bichon would have established itself in the UK before making it in the US. This was not the case. By the time the breed had achieved official recognition in the United States, it had barely set paw on British soil.

One pet dog had been registered with the Kennel Club in 1957, but it wasn't until 1973, when American breeders Mr. and Mrs. Sorstein emigrated to the UK, that a new chapter in the Bichon's history began.

Accompanying the Sorsteins were Rava's Regal Valor of Reenroy and Jenny Vive de Carlisle. These produced two litters, in 1974 and 1975, and formed the foundation of the breed in the UK, with most pedigrees being traced back to these dogs.

The first British breed club, the Bichon Frisé Club of Great Britain, was established in 1974 (recognized by the Kennel Club in 1977), thanks to the efforts of Jackie Ransom (Tresilva) and Eilish M. Banks (Cluneen).

The first show organized by the club was in 1978, and Challenge Certificates (these are needed to make up a Champion) were awarded to the breed for the first time in 1981.

THE BREED TODAY

The last three decades have seen the Bichon emerge as a popular breed. Where at one time it would have been highly unusual to see one— even in the dog press, let alone in the flesh— now the sight of a Bichon Frisé is quite commonplace.

In the United States, there are currently nearly 10,000 registrations per year, making it the 26th

It is easy to see why the Bichon has a worldwide fan club.

most popular dog—a remarkable achievement for such a recent breed to the country. In comparison, more than 2,000 Bichons were registered with the Kennel Club in the UK. Overall, registrations are always smaller in the UK, but, relatively speaking, the Bichon is incredibly successful—it is the third most popular breed in the Toy group (behind the Cavalier King Charles Spaniel and the Yorkshire Terrier), and ranks 19th out of all pedigree dogs.

It isn't difficult to see why the Bichon Frisé is so popular. With his glamorous appearance, convenient size, to-die-for eyes, and loving temperament, the beautiful Bichon wins hearts wherever he goes.

CHAPTER TWO

CHOOSING A BICHON

I t's not difficult to fall in love with a Bichon puppy. Their cuddly-toy appearance, with the white, soft coat, and their large, expressive eyes, makes them very appealing—and very huggable. However much they resemble toys, though, they are not. Resist the temptation to buy one unless you are completely certain that you can attend to his needs for the next 14 years or more.

The Bichon is a very adaptable little dog. He will live happily in a small apartment, or in a castle, provided he is loved and entertained. Many dogs have been littertrained, and do not even need a yard (though walks outside are a must). You do not need a large car if you own a Bichon, and they can easily travel on your lap on public transport. However, the breed does have its own specific needs. Consider the following:

• **Working hours:** Bichons Frisés were bred as companion dogs, and are utterly miserable if left alone for long periods, day in and day out. If you work full-time, and expect to leave the dog at home, think again. No reputable breeder will sell a pup to you, and if you do acquire one, he will soon wreak havoc on your house through boredom and loneliness. If you plan to be out of the house for more than four hours a day, you will have to wait until your circumstances change before you can enjoy the privilege of sharing your life with a Bichon.

• **Time commitment:** As well as being around for your Bichon, he will need training, lots of cuddles, and a great deal of grooming attention. When he is an adult, some regular exercise will also be needed (to stretch his mind as well as his legs). If you are too busy for these commitments, a lower-maintenance breed (or a different species altogether) will be a better choice of pet.

• **Family members:** If you have young children (under the age of five or six years), you should wait before getting a Bichon. The puppies are small and fragile, and could accidentally be injured—even killed—by a child running through the house or dropping them. Kids are accident-prone and sometimes forget to be careful, so don't take any risks. Of course, older children should be respectful of animals and be well behaved before you even consider introducing an animal to the household.

- **Part of the furniture:** How houseproud are you? However much you try to keep a Bichon off the sofa, if that's where he wants to be, he'll find a way of getting there—and he's so mobile, it is very hard to stop him. Life with a Bichon is like living with a cat that you can take for a walk. That means, hair and pawprints on the furniture. If you want to safeguard your expensive three-piece suite, washable throws are essential.

- **Money matters:** Keeping a small breed is often cheaper than keeping larger dogs. Feeding costs and some veterinary treatments, for example, will be less. However, there isn't very much difference—the puppy price will be similar to other breeds, the equipment will be comparable, and so will most veterinary treatments and boarding kennel fees. In addition, there's the cost of professional grooming, if you will not be keeping on top of the coat yourself.

FINDING A BICHON

If you are certain that the Bichon Frisé is the breed for you, it's time to narrow down your search. First, do you want an older dog or a puppy?

Bichon puppies are irresistible, but you need to be sure that you can meet the needs of an adult dog.

An older dog may be a better option, depending on your circumstances.

OLDER/RESCUED DOGS

Older puppies and adult dogs are sometimes available from breeders who have had high hopes for a dog in the show ring that never materialized. Alternatively, you might be interested in a rescued dog.

In both cases, you will usually get a housebroken dog who knows basic house rules and some training commands, and who is just looking for someone to love.

Sadly, there are many Bichons in rescue—usually through no fault of their own. Perhaps they were the beloved companion of an elderly owner who died or went into a nursing home where pets were not allowed.

Many Bichons end up in rehoming centers or breed rescue programs because their owners'

marriages have failed. Divorce usually leads to the sale of the family home, with both people having to find new accommodation (which may not allow pets). Also, if a partner stayed at home to look after the house and family, divorce often means they have to go out to work to help support themselves—and such arrangements usually end up in a very unhappy (and then destructive) Bichon.

Sometimes the arrival of a baby is the cause, or a family member becoming allergic to the dog. As you can see, the Bichon is usually the victim of circumstances beyond his control.

If you are interested in a rescue dog, contact your breed club (details can be sought from your national kennel club) and ask the rescue coordinator for details.

Mary Lee Hess, from Delaware, Ohio, owns two Bichons—Widget (a seven-year-old male) and Lily (a seven-year-old female). Lily is a rescued dog, and here Mary Lee describes the rewards that can come from offering a second chance to a dog in need.

"I was originally attracted to Bichons because of their adorable appearance and the fact that they are nonshedding and hypoallergenic. After I got Widget—who came from a breeder—I soon realized that here was a breed that had many other great attributes too. Bichons have a happy disposition, they are smart, they love being part of a family, and they are great companions.

"My second Bichon, Lily, is a rescued dog. When I was on the internet, I came across a rescue charity called Small Paws Rescue. After reading its website, I decided to become a volunteer—I wanted to be able to help in some way. Lily was my first assignment after I started working for the charity.

"Lily had recently been taken to a rescue shelter near me. My assignment was to offer her a temporary foster home until she could be placed. I went along to pick her up and was met by a skinny, waiflike three-year-old who hadn't been trained or housebroken in any way. The poor little thing didn't even know her name! My heart went out to her. On the ride home, she climbed on to my lap and that was that—I was instantly adopted! Needless to say, Lily's home with me went from temporary foster home to permanent residence!

"It took some time to coax Lily back to full health and confidence. One of the first things I did was bathe and groom her. A sensible diet and a lot of love and patience did the rest.

Once she filled out, received a bit of training, and found her feet in her new home, she settled in incredibly well. She's great friends with Widget and she's bonded so well with me that she hardly leaves my side.

"Lily is definitely a success story, but my experience working for the Small Paws Rescue charity has taught me that it's not always so easy. Some dogs have been 'orphaned' for whatever reason, and these are not too difficult to rehome—they have known a lot of love, they are trained, and they are quite attractive to prospective owners. At the other end of the scale, you see abused or neglected dogs, including those that have come from puppy mills. They have never been out of a cage, and they have no idea what it is like to be loved by an owner.

Lily when she first arrived home.

66 It's vital to find a good match for your lifestyle. 99

It took time and patience for Lily to return to full health and confidence.

"I think that rescue centers are a great way to find a dog, as long as you know what you're letting yourself in for. It's important to be honest with the center about your personal circumstances—it is vital that you find a dog that is a good match for your lifestyle. Some dogs cannot tolerate being left alone for any length of time, and some dogs cannot interact well with children. If you are honest about your lifestyle, the rescue center will do its best to match you with a dog to suit.

"One word of warning I'd offer to anyone thinking of taking on a rescued dog: prepare to have your heart stolen! Lily's given me so much love and affection that I couldn't be without her. Every single day, I think of how much I love her and how grateful I am for having the chance to give her the life she deserves."

Very often, they are completely untrained and unhousebroken. It can take a lot of time and an awful lot of patience to allow the dog to 'warm up' and learn to become a beloved pet. It can take anything from a few weeks to several years to reach this stage, depending on the individual dog and its experiences.

"It's well worth doing though. As I found out with Lily, one of the most rewarding aspects of taking on a rescued dog is seeing them learn to love, trust and enjoy their new life. It's strange, but most rescued dogs seem to know that they've been saved and they thank their new owners with a tremendous amount of affection and loyalty.

Lily and Widget: Devoted companions in a loving home.

Pat with Lucy: A temporary home that became permanent.

Pat and John Parrington from Lancaster, Lancashire, have owned Bichons for 17 years. Experienced show exhibitors and breeders, they were only too willing to volunteer their services when the rescue coordinator's ill health meant that club members were asked to offer foster homes while permanent ones were being sought. Little did they know how their lives would change . . .

"Three years ago, Lucy came into rescue," explains Pat. "Because the coordinator wasn't well at the time, Melvin and I agreed to foster her until she was rehomed. She was about ten years old, and was in quite a state when she arrived. The previous owner had gone into the hospital and a teenager had been caring for her.

"Lucy was very matted and dirty, and her teeth were in a state—I could smell them from several feet away. I had to cut off her coat, and bought her a little jacket to keep her warm. She was only a tiny thing and looked even smaller with no hair.

"The next stage was getting her teeth sorted out. Melvin took Lucy to the veterinarian, but was back with her after an hour as the blood tests showed that her liver and kidney function weren't good enough to cope with the anesthetic needed for the dental.

"Lucy was put on steroids, and we stabilized her enough so that she could go on a drip to have 12 teeth removed.

"A home was found for her, but the people were put off because Lucy was not spayed. Having her teeth out was nerve-wracking enough—let alone risking having her womb removed! At the time, there were several Bichons who were a lot younger who needed a home, so we told the rescue coordinator to rehome the younger dogs, as Lucy was quite happy where she was.

"By this time, Lucy had grown fond of us—especially my husband—and we had grown fond of her, so we decided to keep her. My other dogs (several Bichons, two Shih Tzus, and a Whippet) accepted her quite happily, and now Lucy is top dog, bossing the others about!

"The rescue coordinator's continued ill health meant a replacement was needed, so Melvin and I volunteered. Any dog that needs a home stays with us, or other club members, while a permanent home is found. They stay inside, as part of our family—it's more like fostering, really. We can have as many as three a month, but our other dogs are happy to share their home and family with the newcomers. Lucy is bossy with all of them—but even she is willing to share Melvin's lap with a dog in distress!"

Take time to find a breeder with a reputation for producing typical, healthy puppies.

THE BICHON PUPPY

If you are looking for a Bichon puppy, you can try searching on the internet or you can contact your national kennel club for details of breed clubs. Both the American Kennel Club and the UK Kennel Club have breeder-referral facilities on their respective web sites. If you contact the secretaries of breed clubs, you will need to ask about breeders with litters available (or forthcoming). Ask if the people can be personally recommended—if they have a good reputation in the breed.

Visiting dog shows is another lead. After judging, chat to the exhibitors, and ask those whose dogs you admire whether they are planning a litter. Or perhaps they could recommend people who have dogs similar to their own.

Once you have a list of names, it's time to get interviewing! Don't just pick the first name on the list and buy the first puppy available. It pays to be discerning. This puppy will share your life for many years, and will soon become an integral member of your family—spending some weeks locating the ideal dog is certainly worthwhile.

Call the breeders and then list them in order of preference. You should establish the following:

- How long has the person been breeding?
- How many litters do they produce each year? (The lower the better.)
- What are their reasons for breeding? (To improve their own breeding line, or as a money-making venture?)
- Are the puppies reared in the home? Avoid kenneled dogs, who will not be properly socialized to household sights and sounds.

Watch the mother with her puppies to get an idea of temperament.

- Do they own the dam, and can she be seen when the litter is viewed?
- What after-sales service is provided? Caring breeders will want their dogs back so they can rehome them personally if your circumstances change in the future (whatever age the dog is), and will be glad to give you advice whenever you need it—for the life of the dog.
- What interest does the breeder show in you? A caring breeder will be very fussy about where his or her puppies go, and will ask lots of questions about your lifestyle, family and dog experience. Some even insist on a home-check, and will want to meet everyone who will be living with the puppy.

MEETING THE PUPPIES

Once you've found a breeder who has passed the initial stage of questioning, it's time to meet in person. Try to fortify yourself before you go—it's very easy to be full of good intentions but for it all to be lost when you see a drop-dead gorgeous puppy!

- Double-check that the pups are reared indoors.
- Is the area clean?
- Is the mother friendly? She may be a little protective of her pups, but should not be aggressive in any way.
- Is the mother affectionate and relaxed with the breeder?
- Are the pups lively and inquisitive? If they are sleepy from having just been fed, arrange to view them another time.

- Are the pups clean, with no evidence of parasites in the coat?
- It's important to see the pups together. If the breeder keeps the pups out of sight, and fetches one for you to view, you are not able to assess whether that pup is smaller than his siblings. It is also important to see how the puppies interact and play with each other, so that you can avoid a nervous or aggressive dog.
- A healthy Bichon puppy should be nicely plump (not fat or with a potbelly—which may be a sign of worms). He should have clean eyes, nose, ears and rear end. Any discharges or signs of soreness may indicate poor health.

CHOOSING THE SEX

It's difficult to make generalizations, as every Bichon is an individual, but it's often said that bitches have the brains and boys have the beauty! Some claim that males tend to have softer, gentler temperaments, although females are also very loving.

Ultimately, it's a question of personal taste. Some people always stick to bitches; others to dogs. Your choice may depend on whether you have any dogs already. Two bitches may clash, so it's better to have two males, or, even better, one of each sex (provided you neuter, to avoid unwanted litters—see page 68).

If you choose a female, there are seasons to consider, unless you get her spayed. She will come in "heat" approximately every six months.

Fortunately, with a small breed such as the Bichon, it is relatively easy to keep females away

Male or female? It all comes down to personal preference.

The breeder will help you to choose the puppy that is most likely to suit your lifestyle.

from other dogs during this time, as she can be carried in public places. However, you need to bear in mind that you will have to be very vigilant—your Bichon bitch may well try to escape to find a mate! Extra care should be given to keeping doors and gates closed, and to supervising her when she is in the yard.

Seasons do not just affect females, however. Males, too, will try to wander off to find a bitch, if they remain entire. They may also cock their leg excessively, which can be a nuisance. There are many health benefits to neutering, as well as the issue of convenience, so it should be seriously considered. For more information, see page 68.

SHOW DOG

If you are interested in a puppy for exhibition purposes, you must notify the breeder from the outset. Do not think that you will get a cheaper dog if you keep your intentions secret—you will end up with a good-quality, loving pet dog, who will probably never win anything in the ring. A Bichon with show potential has particular qualities—in body and character—which pet dogs do not have. If you go on to show a dog intended to be a pet, the breeder's good name could well be jeopardized.

Of course, there are no guarantees—even if you purchase a dog with show potential, he may not mature as hoped, or he may not enjoy being shown. However, your chance of success will be higher if you start off with a promising pup.

You may have to wait longer to get a show-quality pup. If puppies have the "wow" factor, the breeders are likely to keep them for themselves! Generally, a Bichon with show potential will have the following qualities:

- Outgoing temperament
- Will readily come to you
- Accepts new experiences easily.
- At eight weeks is in correct proportion for the Breed Standard (see Chapter Seven, "Seeking Perfection")
- Good pigmentation—black nose, good haloes (surrounding the eyes), complete black eye rims and black lips
- Pads should be showing a fair amount of color and preferably be black
- Broad skull with correct head proportions
- Soft, thick coat—should be white, but apricot patches are acceptable as a puppy

If you plan to show your Bichon, you will need to assess conformation as well as character.

- Correct tail set and carriage
- But above all—attitude, attitude, attitude

THE LONG WAIT

When you've picked the puppy you want, and have paid your deposit, there will usually be some delay before the pup is ready to leave the mother and littermates. This time can seem like a lifetime—but preparing for the puppy will keep you busy until you can finally bring him home.

Shopping

- **Crate:** These indoor cages are incredibly useful for puppies and adults alike, both for car travel and as a safe haven and bed in the home. The large ones can be expensive, but a Bichon needs only a smaller size—big enough for an adult dog to turn around in easily. For details of crate-training, see page 34.
- **Bedding:** Fleecy veterinary-type bedding can be costly, but it lasts for years, is soft and absorbent, is machine-washable and dries quickly. Buy two pieces, so you always have a spare (while one is in the wash, for instance).
- **Collar and lead:** Traditional, flat collars tend to knot the Bichon coat, so buy a soft-leather rolled collar and a matching lead. Make sure the collar is adjustable, so you don't have to keep buying a new one as the puppy grows.
- **Bowls:** Stainless steel bowls last for years; they can't break (unlike ceramic bowls), and

Puppy toys must be able to withstand chewing.

they don't scratch easily, which can make the nose sore (like the plastic ones). Buy two—one for food and one for water.

- **Food:** Ask the breeder what food the pup is being fed, and get a supply in. It's important not to change the diet when you first get the puppy, as, coupled with the stress of moving home, it can cause tummy upsets.
- **Grooming equipment:** This can be costly, but if you buy a high-quality brand and look after it, it should last a lifetime. You will need the following:
  - Greyhound comb (two sizes of teeth)
  - Soft slicker brush
  - Nail clippers (guillotine-type is preferred)
  - Small pair of round-nosed scissors (for cutting hair away from the eyes)
  - Hair dryer
  - Nonslip mat for placing the dog on.
- **Toys:** The dog toy market is extensive. It's important to check for safety before purchasing—avoid anything that can be chewed to pieces easily, or has parts that can be swallowed. It may also be worth checking out the cat-toy section of your pet shop, as Bichons like stalking and pouncing on their toys rather as a cat would.
- **Chews:** Puppies need to chew, and if you don't provide them with things with which to satisfy this instinct, they will find their own—such as a chair leg! Avoid colored chews, which stain the coat.

Veterinary registration

If you are not already registered with a veterinarian, you should find one before you bring your puppy home. Ask the advice of dog-owning friends, who may be able to give personal recommendations (or tell you whom to avoid!). Visit a few veterinarians in the area before making your final choice.

- Are the veterinarians and support staff friendly, open and approachable?
- What are the opening hours?
- Is there an appointment system, a turn-up-when-you-want approach, or a bit of both?
- What emergency cover is provided?
- What facilities are offered?
- Is it part of a group of practices? If so, would you have to travel elsewhere for some procedures?

- Are the premises clean?
- Is the waiting room large enough to find a quiet corner, away from other animals? If your Bichon takes a dislike to another dog while waiting for an appointment in a crowded reception space, it can be stressful trying to keep two "enemies" apart.
- Is there sufficient parking and/or good public transport access?

Puppy-proofing

Making your home safe for the new arrival is a top priority. Don't put this job off, thinking you can do it once he's home—it takes seconds for an inquisitive puppy to chew through an electrical cable or fall from a windowsill, so make sure it is a safe place before he sets foot (paw) in the door.

Bichon puppies are great explorers, so make sure your home and garden are as safe as possible.

- Fit baby gates at the bottom of the stairs, and at the entrance to any room to which you want to bar his access.
- Put all toxic chemicals and household detergents out of reach. Medicines should also be stored away in a high cupboard.
- Remove all trailing electrical wires, breakable ornaments, houseplants, etc.
- Shoes are irresistible to a teething puppy, so make room for them in the bottom of a closet or a similar safe place.
- Get into the habit of keeping the toilet lid down. Not only will this prevent a curious puppy from falling into it, but it will prevent him being poisoned if you have recently used a cleaner on it, or if you have a flushable toilet block fitted.
- In the garden, avoid pesticides (such as slug pellets), which can be fatal. If you have to use weed killers and other chemicals, buy only pet-safe ones, and read the labels carefully before use. Keep them out of the puppy's reach at all times.
- Check your yard fencing for any holes at the bottom, which a tiny pup could crawl through.
- Puppies can drown in very little water, so fill in ponds, or fence around them securely so the puppy cannot venture in.
- Many plants (indoors and out) can be toxic to pets. Check the list below, and you can also use a reliable search engine to look for lists of culprits on the Internet.

COLLECTION DAY!

Finally the day will come when it is time to bring your puppy home. Arrange to pick him up from the breeder in the morning—this will

---

HORTICULTURAL HAZARDS

Below is a list of some of the household and garden plants that can be poisonous to dogs. This list is by no means definitive. Ask your local garden center for information on plants before bringing them home.

- Amaryllis
- Azalea
- Cyclamen
- Daffodil
- Dumb cane (Dieffenbachia)
- Elderberry
- Foxglove
- Holly
- Hyacinth
- Iris
- Laurel
- Lily of the Valley
- Milkweed
- Mistletoe
- Nightshade
- Oleander
- Philodendron
- Poinsettia
- Primrose
- Ragwort
- Rhododendron
- Spider plant
- Stinging nettle
- Wisteria
- Yew

It is time for your pup to leave his littermates and start a new life.

give him a good length of time to get to know you, and his new family and surroundings, before nightfall (and so he should settle more easily).

Although a crate is recommended for car travel, for the first journey home, it may be kinder to let him sit on a warm lap, being cuddled. Being separated from his mother and siblings may be traumatic for him; being loved and reassured will help to soothe him.

Of course, you cannot comfort a pup and drive, so enlist the help of a friend or family member for the day—where puppies are concerned, you shouldn't be short of willing volunteers!

Take plenty of strong paper tissues with you in case the pup has an accident or is sick on the journey. If the journey is a long one, then water and a bowl should also be taken.

When you collect the pup, don't forget the paperwork in your excitement! The breeder will have various documents to give you—such as the registration/pedigree papers, a receipt for payment, a diet sheet, and details of any veterinary treatments given (such as worming). Many breeders also provide detailed grooming advice, and other information leaflets.

Once you have everything, it's time for the puppy and you to embark on your new life together. . . .

CHAPTER THREE

ARRIVING HOME

Home at last! You will probably be eager to rush your new Bichon puppy inside and show him his new home, but take him to the yard first. After the journey from the breeder's, he may want to relieve himself and stretch his legs. You can use this opportunity to start his housetraining program—it's never too soon to start!

HOUSEBREAKING

Take your Bichon puppy to the area of the yard that you would like him to use as his regular toileting spot. Ask him to "Get busy" (or whatever command the breeder has already started using with him). If he obliges, repeat the command word (so he learns what it means), give him lots of praise, then let him spend a few minutes exploring the rest of the yard before taking him inside. If he doesn't "go," try again in half an hour or so.

The basic principle of housebreaking is to take the puppy outside so frequently (at least every

two hours) that he doesn't have an opportunity to err. There are certain times when the puppy is more prone to "go":

- First thing in the morning
- After a feeding
- After play/exercise
- When he is excited (by meeting another dog or new visitors).

As well as going outside at these times, he should also be given the opportunity to relieve himself

- before he is settled to bed or for a short daytime sleep;
- if you notice that he is sniffing the ground and shuffling around in a circular motion (a sure sign that he is about to relieve himself).

With time, your puppy will begin to associate the command ("Get busy") with the action (relieving himself). Do not make the mistake of returning inside as soon as the pup finishes his

If you work hard at housetraining in the first few weeks, your pup will soon get the idea.

NOT JUST FOR CATS!

Many Bichons use a litter tray. Put about an inch of fine cat litter in the tray, place it in the crate, and reward him when he uses it, as you would do if he performed outdoors. If your dog learns that this is acceptable, he won't become distressed if he can't hold on through the night, and the tray can also be used if the weather is very bad and he won't venture out.

Do make sure that the tray is scooped out regularly, replacing the litter and cleaning the base with a pet disinfectant.

Warning: Initially, for at least a week, let the puppy near the tray only if he is supervised. If he shows any inclination to eat the cat litter, you will not be able to use it.

business (unless he wants to go indoors). He should be rewarded for being good by having a game with you in the garden (yard), or having a little run about. If you go inside straight away, and he wants to stay and play, he will dread the action of relieving himself, knowing that it will signal the end of his time outside. Many dogs learn to cross their legs and hold on for as long as possible when taken outside for this very reason!

Rained out

Bichons like their creature comforts, so if it is cold or raining, they may be reluctant to brave the bad weather, and would much prefer to use the warm house as a toilet instead.

Is there a covered area, such as an outdoor porch, that you could use? If not, take an umbrella with you and hold it over the puppy. Dry him well when you return indoors, and give him extra-special praise and a treat if he relieves himself in inclement conditions—he will soon realize that it is worth his effort! If you have a very water-phobic dog, you can take him to his indoor litter tray instead (see page 32).

Puddle patience

You will be surprised at how quickly your Bichon puppy learns to be clean in the house, but do not have overly high expectations. It takes some time for your puppy's bladder and bowel to communicate with his brain. Accidents *WILL* happen—so there's no point in getting irate if he slips up. Just clear up the mess with a nonammonia cleaner (pet shops sell special cleaners for the job), and be aware that the pup may return to this area again in the future. Watch him closely, and call him outside if you suspect he needs to go—you need to teach him to associate relieving himself with his outdoor toilet spot, rather than his preferred indoor one.

Whatever you do, *NEVER* rub the puppy's nose in his mess, or shout at or smack him. Such cruelty will teach him nothing. He will not associate something he may have done an hour ago, or even five minutes ago, with your wrath. The only thing he may learn is that you are unpredictable and that he cannot trust you. If you catch him in the act, just encourage him outside, and give him lots of praise and a reward for finishing the job where he should.

TIME AFTER TIME

If your puppy keeps having accidents, try the following:
- Take him outside much more frequently—every half hour if necessary.
- Make sure all accident "hot spots" in the house have been cleaned thoroughly. If they still attract your puppy, move the furniture or put a large (safe) houseplant there instead to bar his access to this area.
- If this doesn't work, get him checked by a veterinarian in case there is an underlying medical cause for his incontinence.
- Review his outside toilet area. If it is on gravel, for example, perhaps he doesn't like the feel of it under his paws—try a soft, grassy area instead.

WELCOME HOME!

Having given the puppy the chance to relieve himself, it's time to show him his new home. Rather than overwhelming him with the sights, sounds and scents of an unfamiliar environment, together with the resident dog bounding over to investigate and the family cat swearing at him, not to mention any children in the family rushing over and fussing over him, take things slowly.

Ideally, you will have collected the puppy early in the morning, while the children are at school. Next, make sure one room in the house is pet-free (ideally the room with his crate in—see page 34), and let your puppy familiarize himself with this area. Once he has had a good sniff about, introduce him to his crate. He may be too excited to settle, but, within the next couple of hours, he will probably need a snooze.

You can take a towel or a blanket to the breeder prior to picking up your puppy. When you bring your puppy—and his blanket—home he will have something that smells familiar.

THE GREAT CRATE

- A week or two before you collect your puppy, it is a good idea to contact the breeder to ask him or her to place a towel or a blanket in with the dam and pups. Alternatively, you could take along your own towel/blanket and ask the breeder to use that instead. When you collect the puppy from the breeder, collect the towel too—it will have picked up the scent of the litter and will provide some comfort for the puppy in the first few days that he is away from his mother and littermates. It will make the puppy's crate seem more like home.

- Make sure there is also an area, away from the bed, which is just covered with newspaper (puppies hate to relieve themselves near their beds, and for the first few weeks, he is unlikely to last through the night without relieving himself).

- Place the puppy's food and water bowl in the crate, together with a safe chew and/or toy.

- Leave the crate door open, and it won't be long before he ventures inside to investigate. With all these wonderful, welcoming goodies, the puppy will think he's stumbled across the perfect puppy pad, and will quickly settle—especially if he is fed in there too.

Put the puppy in his crate for short naps during the day (like babies, puppies need a lot of sleep to assimilate all the information they are learning about the world), and at night. You can then sleep soundly, knowing the pup isn't chewing your dining room chair legs or any electrical cords.

The crate will also help your puppy cope on his own for short periods. Bichons love, love, love people, and spending all day with an owner creates a close bond. The trouble is, sometimes a dog can become over-dependent, and unable to cope if he is left even for a short time. Giving your dog a place that he can call his own, which he associates with warmth, food and comfort, will mean he looks forward to retiring to his crate—and he shouldn't feel worried if you are out of sight.

Because you want the puppy to view his crate as a pleasurable place to spend time, it should never be used as a punishment cell—somewhere you put your Bichon if he has been naughty. Nor should it be used for long periods of time. The crate should be confined to nighttime use, and for occasional short periods during the day.

MEET THE FAMILY

Cat chat
The crate is a great asset when it comes to introducing your Bichon puppy to cats in the home.

- Put your puppy in his crate, and then let the resident cat into the room. Ever since he first arrived, she has probably been very curious to find out more. With the puppy safely confined, she will be able to investigate without fear, and will soon realize that this small bundle of fur isn't a threat to her.
- After a couple of these visits, it's time for a face-to-face meeting. It's best to choose a time of the day when the puppy is quiet and calm, such as after a feeding.
- Choose a room where the cat has an upward escape route (e.g., to the back of the sofa). Bring the puppy in, and the cat will investigate in her own time, when she feels confident.
- If the pup oversteps the mark and is too boisterous, a quick hiss and a stern look from puss usually sends a pup running in fear, and he will learn to be more respectful at the next meeting.

Usually, Bichons and cats become close friends. The Bichon is a very feline dog himself. He grooms himself (and his pals) like a cat, he is agile, and he loves his creature comforts. He is tactile, stalks his playmates in a catlike way, can be litter-trained very easily, and uses his paws to open doors. In fact, the Bichon has often been described as the ideal breed for a cat lover who wants to take something for a walk! Because of their similarities, and comparable size, cats and Bichons soon come to an amicable agreement, and usually become good companions.

Canine chums
The Bichon is also easygoing with other dogs, although he can become a little jealous if too much attention is conferred on a companion and he feels left out!

- Use the yard to introduce a Bichon puppy to a resident dog, as there will be fewer territorial issues there than indoors. If you are taking on an older dog who is fully vaccinated, a park is the preferred location, as it will serve as neutral ground for both dogs.

RAINING CATS AND DOGS

Maureen Reynolds from Redditch, Worcestershire, has been a lifelong cat owner. Cats fulfilled all the requirements she wanted in a pet—apart from one, for which she needed a dog. . . .

"In 1984, I realized I wanted something I could take for a walk," says Maureen. "I have only had one cat who would come for walks, but none of the others would oblige, so my husband, John, and I decided that we'd look for a dog.

"John is allergic to fur, and suffers from asthma, so we needed a nonshedding breed. I've always liked white dogs. A friend has Samoyeds, and I was tempted to get a Japanese Spitz, but at that time, the temperaments were not very good in the UK, so we did some more research.

REIGN OF TERROR

"After seeing some Bichon litters and reading about the breed, I was put in contact with a breeder, who had a litter of puppies and a 12-month-old bitch. We decided that the only thing better than one Bichon was two, so we bought Opal, an eight-week-old pup, and Penny, a year-old show dog.

"Fred, my mixed-breed cat, terrorized Penny at first. If she was on my lap, and Fred wanted to be there, he would flick her ears with his paw, and she would go rigid with fear. She was too scared to move.

"But Opal, who was introduced to Fred as a puppy, wasn't scared of Fred one bit. If she wanted to oust him from my lap, she would close her eyes tight and then push him out of the way with her bottom. Even if he clouted her, she would just keep persisting!

Bichons are very cat-like, and most live happily with a feline friend.

Sapphire, a Birman, is delighted when there is a litter of puppies to play with.

CAT-LIKE DOGS

"I chose Bichons as they are so catlike. They use their paws like cats, play like them, wipe their faces clean, stalk each other and even knead you like a cat. I think Opal thought she was a cat. She would watch Fred jump halfway up the fence and then walk up the remaining part to the top, and she would try too. Of course, not having a cat's retractable claws, she just slid back down!

"After Fred, I got Amber and Sapphire, two Birmans, followed by the Bichons, Puppy and Cindy. Sapphire loves being mugged by the dogs. They leap all over her. She's never had hair on the tips of her ears, as the dogs are always licking them clean for her! She adores being with the dogs, and will even call for them.

"The cats especially like it when we have a litter of puppies, and will snuggle in with them in the whelping box. When I call all the dogs to be groomed, the Birmans trot along to have their hair done too!

FAN CLUB

"We now have a white British Shorthair, called Alley. She's not as fond of the dogs as the Birmans, but the Bichons adore her. All the dogs are very 'helpful' if any one of the cats has a fur ball. When coughing up the hair, the Bichons pile in, with their noses in the cat's ear or under the tail, as if they are trying to assist!

"The cats and dogs are very similar to each other, and I love them all to bits. The only difference is that Bichons don't purr!"

If you are tactful with introductions, Bichons will quickly learn to enjoy each other's company.

- The two dogs may have had an initial introduction, as most breeders insist on meeting all family members (canine and human) before agreeing to sell one of their pups. The same is true of rescue organizations.
- Unless either of the dogs is particularly boisterous, keep them off the lead, as dogs are more relaxed when free. They can then talk to each other in canine language (using their body as well as their "voices") and establish who is the higher ranking of the two (in most cases, the older dog—although not always).
- Do not interfere with the dogs unless you fear for their safety. Growling may sound terrible to a human ear, but is a basic form of communication to dogs.
- In most cases, the two dogs will be playing with each other within minutes—although it will take a few weeks for them to settle fully.

- You may find that the pup will become cheekier or more challenging as he matures, testing how far he can push the other dog. Again, they will soon sort themselves out. However, if there is an ongoing problem between them, seek professional advice (your veterinarian can point you in the right direction).
- Make sure the puppy doesn't constantly pester the resident dog, particularly if the dog is quite elderly. The dog may feel obliged to keep up, when really he wants to rest, or he could snap through impatience.
- Do not let the novelty of a new puppy affect your relationship with the older dog, who will need reassurances that he is still loved dearly. When the pup is enjoying a snooze in his crate, take the older dog for a walk and enjoy some high-quality time together.

The people pet

As well as being introduced to the household pets, the puppy will also need to meet his human family. By the time the children return from school, your Bichon should already be feeling at home—familiar with his crate, the layout of the floor(s) he is allowed on, and with you.

Keep the meeting calm. Screaming, over-excited children can make a terrific din, which, to a dog's sensitive hearing, can be very upsetting. The puppy needs to know that these little people are his family, and that they are fun and loving. If he's scared of them, it can be an uphill struggle to persuade him to change his mind.

- Play must be gentle and controlled, and the puppy should be picked up only if the child is seated (if dropped, a Bichon can sustain terrible injuries).
- Show children how to pet in an acceptable way—to stroke the puppy gently rather than to pat in a heavy-handed manner.
- Make sure that the puppy gets plenty of rest. A child's batteries may never run out, but a pup needs naps to recharge.
- When he is in his crate/bed, or when feeding, the puppy should not be disturbed. The pup must learn that his crate is a quiet, child-free haven that he can retire to whenever he needs time alone.
- It's only natural that a child will want to share his snack with the puppy, or to sneak food from his plate to drop it on the floor for him. Explain why this is not allowed—it will encourage the dog to beg, and will also make him prone to obesity, which can be detrimental to his health.
- Depending on your children's ages, involve them in different aspects of caring for the puppy. Perhaps one child could help prepare his food with you, or groom him. Fun training exercises, games, and walks make great family activities (although young children should not be allowed to hold on to the lead near roads or other places that can pose a danger).

It's important that puppies are socialized with children, as they will encounter "little people" in everyday life when you are out and about. If you do not have any children, ask friends, neighbors or family members to bring their families along to meet the puppy—you don't usually have to ask twice! However, give the puppy a few days to settle into his home first. The pup needs to get to know his immediate family before he is bombarded with new faces.

NAME

If you chose the puppy's name when you first selected him from the litter, then the breeder may have already started getting him used to it. If you still haven't made up your mind, try to decide soon—or the puppy will start to think that his name is Puppy!

Use the name as often as you can: when calling the puppy, when cuddling him, and while he's eating. It's important that he associate his name with enjoyable experiences—if you use it only before telling him off, he is less likely to respond to his name in the future!

Not believing they could have children, Belgian couple Rita and Johan Douwen poured all their love into their "canine kids" but when the stork came calling, they had plenty of love left to give their two-legged Bichons too.

"Our story starts in June 1990 when I went to see newborn puppy Lady. She is the one who started it all. With her, I started to show and learned how to groom. In 1992, I got my first boy, Hermelino, who came from Germany. Together we were a winning team. He is a Champion in seven countries, is a Best in Show winner and also Vice World-winner.

"In 1993, I had my first litter from which I kept a female, Rhanna. We were another winning team, as we won seven Championship titles, Vice World-winner, and, together with Hermelino, many Best Braces. At this time, my husband (Johan) and I knew that having a child of our own would be very difficult, so our Bichons became rather like children to us. But, in 1996, just after receiving news from England that I would have a new show puppy, Johan and I also got the news that a human baby was on the way!

TRYING TIMES

"As my pregnancy was very difficult, I had to lie down at home a lot. Our Bichons knew there was something wrong with 'Mummy.' They followed me to the bathroom when I was sick, and just sat beside me, licking my hand. When I was on the sofa, Hermelino was always beside me, with his head on my tummy. As this grew

Elyne pictured with the Bichon "gang."

Rhanna, the Bichon, keeping watch over Joryne.

bigger, he would feel the baby kick and would look at me with a funny expression: 'Mum, did you feel that as well?!'

"So the big day arrived! I gave all the dogs a very big hug and went to the hospital where my first daughter, Elyne, was born. Each day, Johan would return home from the hospital with the clothes that she had worn, and the dogs would have a good sniff.

"When I finally came home, I went in first and said hello to the dogs, while Johan undressed the baby. Then he brought her in, and I presented her to the three Bichons; they were so gentle and careful with her—you wouldn't believe it. But when people came over for a visit, all three dogs would sit around the cradle to protect her! Each time she cried, one of them came to me, to let me know!

GROWING FAMILY
"I involved the dogs in everything I did with the baby. Elyne is now seven years old, and even now, when we all go upstairs to bed at night—dogs included—Lady always goes in Elyne's bedroom to check that she is sleeping.

"Next, along came Hamish, who came to us as an eight-month-old puppy. He fitted into our family straight away, but he seemed a little confused by 'the funny little Bichon' on two legs! But he soon found out that when he followed that funny Bichon, he would get a piece of her cookie . . . .

"In 1999, along came Silke, who was born in our house. Elyne really enjoys her; she saw the birth and has seen the litter grow up—though she did get upset when the other puppies had to go.

"In 2000, Dipsy was born. Again, everything was just fine—Elyne and the dogs both respected the rules: when a dog is asleep in his bed, you leave him alone; when he is chewing a bone, you leave him alone; you don't pull at the

Continued overleaf

Elyne has learned to respect both dogs and puppies.

ears or tail . . . . We never had any problems—far from it. Sometimes, when Elyne was a toddler, she would fall asleep cuddled up with Hermelino.

INTENSIVE CARE

"Joryne, our second daughter, was born in 2001. I had the same pregnancy problems as with Elyne, so the dogs were already prepared for what would happen—except this time, there were problems. Joryne had complications after her birth and had to go into intensive care. So when I got home from the hospital, the dogs were very confused because 'Mum' was back, but there was something missing! The three oldest Bichons were really looking for the baby, so when she finally got home three weeks later, they were so happy.

"My oldies play a little bit less with our girls now, but they are 14, 13 and 12 years old. In 2002, Minty came along, so now we have six Bichons in the house. Minty was nine months old when she arrived and had never lived with a child. But she and Silke are always playing with Joryne—they just adore her.

BICHON CUDDLES

"Each day, when it is 12 P.M. and 3:30 P.M., they start getting restless, knowing that this is the time I get Joryne from the nursery, and then Elyne from school. Sometimes, I take one of the dogs with me to collect the children. The Bichons love all those little hands at the nursery/school gates, and everyone wants to cuddle them! Whenever I have puppies, I always take one along, so that they can get used to the attention of lots of children.

"My kids learn a lot from growing up with dogs. They have seen puppies being born, and they also understand that living things can get sick and die. We are already preparing Elyne for the fact that, one day, we may lose Lady or Hermelino. They also know to respect the animals—especially as we have three senior dogs in the family.

"As Elyne is getting older now, she is helping me with the dogs, feeding them, letting them out in the garden, and she even tries to groom them. But when Joryne takes the brush—the Bichons are gone!"

FIRST NIGHT

The first few nights that a puppy spends in his new home can be sleepless ones. Although fatigue can make people irritable, try to consider things from the puppy's point of view. Until now, he has slept in the only bed he has ever known, surrounded by his mother and littermates, and with the familiar smells of home and of his human family. Now, he is in a strange place and is expected to settle all alone. Is it any wonder that puppies are fretful at first?

- Because you have spent the day with the puppy, settling him into his new home, and introducing him to his crate, he should feel safe and secure in his "den." It helps if you put something in his bedding that smells of his previous home, such as a blanket, towel or safe toy from the breeder (see page 34).

- You might want to put the crate in your bedroom, or in a room close by, so you can reassure the puppy if he wakes in the night. Often, a soft, friendly voice is all that is needed to settle a pup. But be careful that the pup does not wear down your defenses, and worm his way into your bed!

- Once a Bichon has shared a bed with you, he will feel very put out if he can't sleep there every night, so think carefully before acting. If you know you are a pushover, it may be best to keep him in his crate downstairs. He may be a little upset at first, but he will soon get used to the routine and accept it.

The puppy's first night away from his mother and littermates is bound to be tough.

- If you have a resident dog, your Bichon will find comfort in having him close by, once they have got to know each other.

- Allow the puppy to relieve himself before you put him in the crate, and, if you are not going to have the crate in your bedroom, leave a radio on in the room (at a low volume and tuned to an all-night talk station).

- A ticking clock may help a pup to settle, as it is reminiscent of his mother's heartbeat.

- Some people advocate putting a warm hot-water bottle wrapped securely in a towel, so the pup can snuggle up to it. Do make sure it can't be chewed, though, and do not use hot water inside it, as it could burn his skin.

- Remember, although the initial nights may be very disturbed, your Bichon will soon settle. Come daybreak, everything will seem brighter, and when you cuddle up to your gorgeous puppy, you will quickly forgive him for the nighttime whines and howls.

CHAPTER FOUR

EARLY LESSONS

The Bichon may not be the first breed that comes to mind when you think of dog training, but they are actually very good pupils. Although they don't come from a working background, they are "people pets," who, for centuries, have been devoted companions. As such, they get a great thrill from pleasing their owners—which is half the battle won!

BASIC PRINCIPLES

- Keep it fun! If you hammer away at training for hours on end, repeating the same thing over and over again, your Bichon will get bored and will switch off. It won't be much fun for you, either. Keep sessions short and sweet, practicing little and often.
- Make it worthwhile. Although Bichons love to please, most need a little more motivation. A tasty treat (deducted from the daily food allocation), praise and lots of cuddles will all help to persuade your dog to give his best.

- Find the treats that work best for your dog. They shouldn't be messy to hold; they should be cut into small cubes (to give enough of a taste but not to take forever to chew and swallow), and should be very desirable to your dog. Some dogs love cubes of cheese, others sausage or ham—it depends on the individual dog. You might want to reserve your Bichon's favorite treat only for when he is learning something new, or for when he needs that extra boost for difficult exercises.
- Reward good behavior (above), but ignore inappropriate behavior. Shouting and smacking are big no-nos. Getting cross will just confuse your dog, and he will be more apprehensive in future training sessions. If you are learning a new language, you wouldn't expect a tutor to hit you across the nose with a rolled-up newspaper just because you got a verb conjugation wrong, would you?!
- Start with the basics and progress slowly. For example, if you are teaching your Bichon to

Make training fun so that your Bichon wants to do as you ask.

JOIN A CLASS

The basic exercises of pet obedience are included in this chapter, but it's still important to enroll in a puppy-training class. Not only will you be shown exactly what to do, and given specific guidance if you are experiencing any difficulties, but it's also a very good socializing experience for your Bichon.

However . . . do not just sign up for the first class you find. Visit without your dog initially, to observe that the class is well organized and that the instructors use only positive, reward-based methods (no yelling, choke chains, etc.).

beg, reward him for lifting one paw—it's a step in the right direction! If you are teaching the Stay exercise, don't expect your dog to sit and stay for 10 minutes when you are out of sight. One step away, for three seconds, is a good starting point, and you can build up gradually from there.

• Your choice of location is vital. When starting off a new exercise, your Bichon needs to concentrate. A quiet room is ideal. When the exercise has been mastered, then practice it outside in the yard, and finally in a park (provided your Bichon is old enough) where there are lots of distractions.

CLICKER TRAINING

The clicker is a great tool in your training kit. This small plastic box makes a "click" when pressed with your thumb. It has been described as a "yes marker," telling your dog when he does something that is desirable. In the beginning, the click is followed by a treat, and, through association, the dog learns that a reward is coming—be it immediately, or, later in his training, as long as 20 minutes after the click. In fact, eventually, the dog will associate the click itself as being a reward.

If you are interested in this type of training, join a club/class where it is the preferred method. Clicker training is so popular now, you shouldn't have any difficulty locating one near you.

If you do not want to use the clicker, you can adapt the exercises below by just giving a reward and praise for behavior you want to encourage.

- If your Bichon just doesn't understand an exercise, take a step back, return to the beginning and start again. Always end on a positive note, with an exercise you know your Bichon can do easily. This guarantees he will finish with a reward and lots of praise. Ending on a failure casts a shadow on the whole session.

- Young puppies are excellent pupils. Don't believe people who say that you can't begin to teach a puppy to sit or to come until he is six months old. By then, he will be hitting adolescence and will be more difficult than he ever was as a youngster. Pups are naturally inquisitive and are eager to learn, so start as soon as you get your baby Bichon home.

SIT

- The easiest way to teach this exercise is to hold a treat just above the dog's head, so he will look up to get it. Then, bring the treat back a little more, to just behind the dog's

Sit is a simple exercise to teach.

Use a treat to lure your Bichon into the Down.

The pup will soon realize that the only way to get the treat is to go into the Down.

nose. To reach it, he will have to put his bottom on the floor. As soon as he does, click, give him the treat, and then praise him.

- Practice little and often and your Bichon will go into the Sit position as soon as you hold your hand above his head. This is the time to introduce the command "Sit." If you use the command before the pup understands what the exercise is about, he will think the word means "jump up to get the treat" or "scratch your ear," or whatever he was doing instead of sitting!

- In time, you can stop using the hand signal, and can simply ask your dog to sit.

- As your Bichon becomes more and more proficient, you can begin to reduce the number of clicks, so you will give the sound only for the fastest response.

- The Sit exercise can be practiced throughout the day: just before your Bichon is given his meal, before you put his lead on, or before you open the door.

DOWN

This is a very useful exercise for the Bichon owner. Once your dog can lie down on command, it makes grooming the tummy and other difficult-to-reach places a lot easier.

- Getting your Bichon to lie down is taught in the same way as the Sit, but, this time, hold the treat to the ground.

- It may take the puppy a short while to figure out how to get the treat, and he will try all sorts of positions to get it. Make sure you do not release the treat from your hand until his tummy is touching the ground.

RECALL TRAINING

Recruit an assistant when you are training your Bichon to come. As you call "Come" the assistant releases the dog, and you are ready to give lots of praise and a treat when the dog runs to you.

- Click as soon as the pup is in the right position, give him the treat, and tell him what a clever puppy he is.
- As before, introduce the word "Down" when he is reliably going into position. When he understands the command, try it without the hand signal.
- Don't confuse your Bichon by telling him "Down" when you want him to get down from the sofa. Otherwise, he'll think you want him to lie down on the settee! Instead use a different command, such as "Off."

COME

Bichon puppies are like little shadows—most rarely wander more than a few paces away from their beloved owners. However, don't take this for granted. As your puppy grows, he will become more independent, and if you want to be able to let him off the lead in the park when he is older, it is important to know that he will always come straight back when you call.

- Sit on the floor, a few steps from your puppy. Call him to you, and click and treat him when he comes. If you use a high-pitched tone of voice, and say "Puppy, Come!" in a very excited way, he should come running. Give lots of praise and a cuddle afterward.
- Repeat this for a brief time and often, increasing the distance between you. If the puppy is slow in coming, be more excited than ever—show him a squeaky toy, or clap your hands to get him to you.
- When your Bichon understands what is required, make it a little more difficult. Hide

behind an armchair or a table and call him. He will feel very clever for finding you!

- Try the recall with your puppy in a different room from you, and then practice in the yard too.
- If, in the yard, your Bichon doesn't respond to your recall, walk off in the opposite direction from him—he will soon come running!
- If your Bichon doesn't reliably come back when you call, don't let him wander off in the park when he is older. Stay close to him, or use an extending lead.

Don't be too ambitious when you start teaching your Bichon to stay.

STAY

Bichons love their owners, and can find the Stay quite difficult. If you are at one end of the yard, that's where they will want to be too. If your Bichon understands that this is just a fun game, and that there will be lots of rewards, praise and cuddles at the end, he should give it his best shot.

Being able to put the brakes on a dog is very useful, and it can be a lifesaver. For example, you can ask your Bichon to stay when you open the car door while you attach his lead, rather than him leaping out of his crate/carrier potentially into a dangerous situation.

- With your Bichon in the Down position, walk a couple of steps in front of him, turn, and give him the Stay hand signal (an outstretched arm, with the palm facing him, fingers pointing to the sky). Dogs are very good at understanding body language, and this signal tells him in no uncertain terms to stay away from you, especially if it is reinforced with a low, stern "Stay." If the pup stays—even for a second—click. Return to him, and give him lots of praise and a treat.
- Increase the level of difficulty very, very slowly. Progress to walking three steps away from the pup, and then, when he will reliably stay on the spot, make him wait for a little longer before you return to him.
- When he understands that staying earns a click, make him wait a little longer before you give it to him. When he is confident, click him at the end of the exercise, when you have walked back to him.

- When your Bichon has mastered the Down-Stay, try the Sit-Stay. If you really want a challenge, put your dog in the Stay and then hide out of sight!
- Staying on the spot is very boring for a puppy, so don't overdo this exercise.

WALKING ON A LEAD

The joy of owning a small breed is that, if the dog pulls, he won't yank your arm out of its socket! In fact, very few Bichons pull; most naturally trot alongside their owners. However, lead-training must be taught to get the puppy used to the sensation of being on a lead (avoiding "bucking bronco" syndrome when he's older). It's also important that your Bichon walk close to you, so he isn't in danger of being stepped on by other walkers on the pavement.

The collar

First of all, get your Bichon puppy used to wearing a collar.

- As with all training, little and often is best.
- Put the collar on, and make sure you can fit two fingers underneath it. If it is any tighter, it will be uncomfortable; if it is looser, it could catch on things, or he could slip out of it when the lead is attached.
- Distract your pup when he is wearing the collar, so he won't try to scratch it off. Play with a toy, or do some easy training together, so he can earn some rewards.
- Put the collar on for just a few minutes throughout the day, to start off with, and he will soon accept it.

> ### BICHON TIP
>
> **R**olled collars, rather than flat ones, do not break the coat hair, so are preferred by most Bichon owners. It is also advisable to opt for a natural leather collar that isn't dyed. Some collars have been known to turn dogs pink, blue or green when they get wet! As a less expensive alternative to leather, you could opt for tubular, braided nylon collars. These are strong, lightweight, found in a variety of colorfast shades, and can be easily cleaned in the washing machine.

- Never leave your puppy unsupervised with the collar on. Accidents can—and do—happen.

The lead

When your Bichon will happily accept wearing a collar, then it's time for phase two—the lead.

- Take your Bichon out to the yard. Make sure he has urinated and/or defecated, and that he has stretched his legs, and then fix the lead to his collar. Walk slowly around the yard, encouraging him to walk with you. Don't pull the lead; just clap your hand to your thigh, or show him a treat in your hand and get him to follow it.
- When your puppy walks a couple of paces next to you, click and treat.
- Traditionally (and for formal obedience), dogs walk on their owners' left-hand sides, but if the right side feels more natural for you, that's fine.
- Practice so that you can click your Bichon after 5 steps next to you, and then ten, and so on.

LEAD-TRAINING

To begin with, your pup will need to get used to wearing a collar and lead.

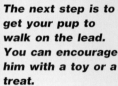

The next step is to get your pup to walk on the lead. You can encourage him with a toy or a treat.

In time, your Bichon will be a pleasure to take on walks.

- Introduce the word "Heel" once he understands the position he should be in.
- If the pup walks ahead of you, or lags behind, do not pull. Not only can it damage a Bichon's neck, but it is likely to encourage him to respond by also pulling. Instead, stop walking, call him to you in a fun, happy tone of voice, put him in the Sit position by your side, and start again.

CAR TRAVEL

It is important to train your Bichon to travel in the car. Most dogs love a trip out, and will soon learn to settle quietly when they are in transit. The best plan is to use a crate or a traveling box, placed in the rear of the car, or secured on the back passenger seat with a safety belt.

- Do not take your Bichon out after he has eaten, or you will risk travel sickness.
- To start with, go for a short journey and stop at the local park where you can give your Bichon a run. In this way, he will associate car travel with doing something he enjoys.

• If your Bichon makes a fuss when he is in the car, simply ignore him. He will soon learn that barking and whining does not produce results.

• When you reach your destination, do not allow the pup to leap out of his crate the moment you open it. Adopt a drill of saying "Wait," fastening on his lead, and then allowing him to come out.

Use a crate when taking your Bichon in the car.

FUN TRICKS

Training does not always need to be serious. Your Bichon will thrive on the mental stimulation of being taught new exercises, and he will enjoy being praised and given a reward. Why not try teaching him some fun tricks, such as sitting up to beg or giving a paw? Bichons love an audience, and you will have something to show off when friends come visiting!

Bichons love to show off, and will enjoy learning tricks to entertain your friends.

CHAPTER FIVE

CARING FOR YOUR BICHON

The Bichon Frisé is one of the most glamorous of all dog breeds, but it takes a good deal of time to keep the coat looking its best. Apart from coat care, the Bichon is fairly low-maintenance; he doesn't require hours of daily walking, and he is rarely fussy about what he eats. His main need is your company and love—which, with a breed as affectionate and fun as the Bichon, is not difficult to give.

DIET

Your Bichon puppy should come with full instructions. The breeder will provide you with a detailed diet sheet, outlining exactly what, and how much, to feed your pup, with information on his changing needs as he grows. This information is likely to have been compiled from years of experience in the specific needs of the Bichon, with the breeder having tried and tested various types of diets. By following their advice, you will save yourself a lot of time and effort in finding the most suitable food.

The other important factor is that a change in diet can cause stress to the puppy's body, resulting in digestive upsets. Even if you intend to change the dog's diet in the long-term, it is important to follow the breeder's recommendations for at least a month, so your Bichon doesn't have to cope with the upheaval of a new home and family, as well as diet, all in one go. If you decide to change the diet, discuss it with your breeder. He or she may be able to recommend a suitable alternative.

Introducing a new diet

Do not change your Bichon's food suddenly. The new food should be introduced gradually, to give your dog a chance to acclimatize to it slowly.

- Start off by adding a tiny amount of the new food to your dog's current food.
- After doing this to his meals for one day, add a little more of the new food.

- Correspondingly give less of the current food. So, if you add a teaspoon of the new food, give a teaspoon less of the other food.
- Over the course of a week to 10 days, you will eventually reach the stage where the dog is being fed solely on the new food.
- If he experiences diarrhea, it is likely that the changeover has been too sudden, or that the new food doesn't agree with him.
- If the diarrhea continues for more than 12 hours, or if the dog shows any other signs of ill health, consult your vet.

Types of food

The pet-food industry is a huge one, with many companies offering different types of food to suit all needs and tastes. Canned meat with biscuits is still popular with some people, although the complete foods have won many fans. These dry foods are so-called because they are nutritionally complete, containing all the nutrients a dog needs. They usually come in various life stages: puppy, adult, and senior, with some companies also offering "working" for active, working dogs, "light" for dogs who need to watch their weight, and even "Toy" varieties for smaller breeds.

It is possible that the breeder will recommend that you avoid food containing beef and beef derivatives. This is not uncommon for white-coated breeds that suffer from skin problems—it is believed that beef and beef derivatives can exacerbate skin conditions in pale-colored dogs. Not all dogs will be affected in this way, but if you have concerns, discuss them with the breeder when you collect your puppy, and then with your veterinarian.

Some dogs are also allergic to wheat, and wheat-free diets are available. If your Bichon develops a skin disorder that may be the result of a food allergy, ask your veterinarian and breeder for advice.

The adult Bichon will need two meals a day.

Number of meals

Again, this should be outlined on the diet sheet. At first, your Bichon puppy will probably be on four meals a day, reducing to three meals at around five months, and then down to two by seven months. Although owners of larger breeds often reduce to one large meal a day, the Bichon is better suited to remaining on two small meals for the rest of his life. With older dogs, in fact, it is sometimes advisable to divide their daily food allowance into three meals, as their digestive system can become sluggish.

EXERCISE

Bichons love their home comforts, and would happily spend all day with you, curled up on the sofa, watching the TV and being petted. Although Bichons don't need huge amounts of exercise, it's important that they get out to stretch their legs and their minds. A Bichon (and owner!) will quickly stagnate mentally if he only gets to see four walls every day.

Until the age of six months, a Bichon puppy needs only two or three daily sessions in the garden to get rid of his excess energy. However, it's still important to take your puppy out to socialize him as soon as he is fully vaccinated. Short lead walks, and also carrying the pup around markets, in bus stations, etc., will ensure that he realizes, from a young age, that the world is a fun, exciting place, not one to be feared.

When your Bichon is older, you can enjoy longer exercise sessions together—a couple of 20-minute walks a day, together with free access to your safe, well-fenced yard.

The Bichon does not require a lot of exercise, but he will appreciate the stimulation of going to new places.

BICHON BLITZ!

Many owners are aware of the "Bichon Blitz"—that time in the early evening when a Bichon transforms into a thing possessed and does wall-of-death around the furniture, and races anywhere and everywhere as if he is being chased by demons. To new owners, this phenomenon can be rather startling, but you will soon get used to it!

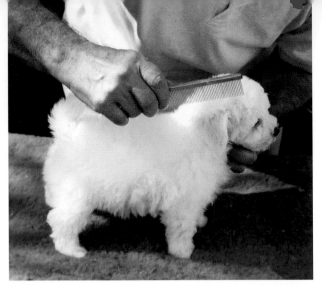

Daily grooming must start from six weeks of age.

- Keep the first sessions short, and end by praising your puppy and giving him a treat.
- Gradually lengthen the sessions, as your puppy learns to accept being handled and groomed, and also introduce Sit and Down training (Chapter Four) to get him in the best position for those difficult-to-reach places on the body.
- Giving your puppy a safe toy to play with or a chew will help to prevent boredom—and might keep him from playing with the brush!

GROOMING

Bichons should be groomed every day from the age of six weeks. The breeder will have started to get the puppy used to being brushed and handled, but it's important that you continue with his or her good work. It is vital that the grooming experience is viewed in a positive light. If the pup associates grooming with pain, discomfort or boredom, he will quickly learn to dread the appearance of his grooming bag. Grooming should be mutually enjoyable for both you and your dog.

- Place your puppy on a nonslip mat when he is relaxed, and stroke him. Talk to him in a calm, loving voice, apply some anti-static spray, and then start to groom him gently with a soft slicker brush (see opposite for tips on the best grooming technique).
- If you encounter any tangles, do not pull on the hair. Instead, hold the offending part of the coat in your fingers, and then brush through the knot, so your pup won't feel any tugging.

Grooming technique

The adult coat starts coming through between seven and 10 months of age (although, in some dogs, it can also change a second time at around 18 months). It often starts to come through at the tail, and finishes with the head. By now, your Bichon should be very relaxed when he is groomed, which will help to ensure that the transition to the thicker, longer coat is as smooth as possible.

- Before you begin, you might want to spray an anti-static solution on the coat. This is not essential, but it can help to prevent the brush from pulling on tangles, and also minimizes damage to the coat.
- First, brush the coat with a soft slicker brush. Part the coat, and go through each section of hair, down to the skin.
- Be methodical and follow the same routine each session, so you don't leave any areas ungroomed. For example, start at the head and move down along the body, finishing with the tail.

BRUSHING AND COMBING

If you take on a Bichon, regular grooming sessions are an essential part of your care regime.

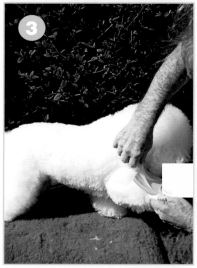

A slicker brush is the best grooming tool to use on the Bichon's coat. It can also be used to tease out mats and tangles.

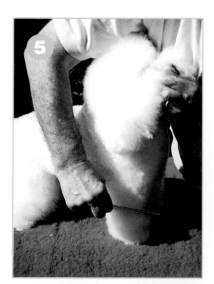

When you have brushed the coat thoroughly, repeat the process with a comb, working through each section of the coat.

- If you encounter knots, brush them out gently, holding the fur as described before.
- Knots gather wherever the coat rubs, notably behind the ears, in the "armpits," and around a dog's genitals.
- When the coat has been brushed thoroughly, go through it again, this time with a comb. If you find more knots, use your brush to remove them.
- Use the comb to lift the hair, to give the coat shape.
- As you groom, check the skin carefully. Hotspots can occur in the breed. Some breeders recommend a natural mouthwash solution, or even cornstarch, which, applied to the red area, helps calm down the heat patch. However, it is a good idea to get any skin abnormalities checked out by your veterinarian first, to make sure it isn't something serious.

Bathing and cleaning

White coats look fantastic when they are clean and sparkling, but Bichons are not quiet, sedentary dogs—they love to roll in the yard and jump in puddles just as most other breeds do! Such activities don't always have to end in a dip in the bath. Again, cornstarch can come to the rescue. If you wash the dog's feet and face, cornstarch can be applied to the coat, and brushed out as the coat is dried.

- If a bath cannot be avoided, groom the dog thoroughly before you start.
- Place a rubber mat in the bath (or a large sink, or even a shower cubicle), so the dog will not slip.

- Use warm—not hot—water to wet the coat thoroughly, right down to the skin.
- Then apply the shampoo, following the manufacturer's instructions. A gentle, natural shampoo often works wonders, and doesn't irritate the skin. If in doubt as to which type to use, ask your breeder.
- Massage the shampoo into a lather, making sure you get down to the roots of the coat.
- Rinse thoroughly and check that there are no hidden suds lurking. Shampoo left in the coat can cause intense itching and irritation.
- Dry the coat with a towel, pressing and squeezing the hair with it (rather than rubbing, which can cause tangles).
- Then dry the coat with a hair dryer, brushing the coat through with the slicker, to help give it volume. If left to dry naturally, the coat will fall into corkscrew curls and make the dog look more like a Bolognese than a Bichon Frisé.
- Until the dog learns to stand still and accept being dried, you might need another pair of hands to hold and amuse him while you get on with operating the hair dryer.

Scissoring

Scissoring is something of an art form. Many pet owners take their dogs to a groomer every three months, but some learn to do it themselves. Scissoring tidies up the coat and follows the natural contours of the dog's body. Your dog's breeder may give you advice, and most breed clubs run grooming seminars to show inexperienced owners how to get a professional look without having to pay professional prices.

BATHING

A white coat looks spectacular, but you will have to work hard to keep it that way...

Soak the coat thoroughly with warm water.

Work the shampoo into a rich lather.

Rinse the coat until there is no trace of shampoo.

Wrap your Bichon in a towel to absorb excess moisture.

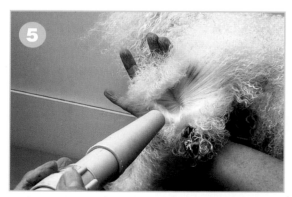

If you use a dryer, make sure it is on a moderate setting.

The coat should be groomed as it dries.

SCISSORING

It takes many years to develop the expertise to scissor a Bichon coat for show ring presentation.

1 The front is scissored to give a clean, smooth outline.

2 Trimming around the paws.

3 Working along the line of the shoulders.

4 The coat along the back should be like a close-fitting jacket.

5 The underside should present a neat curve.

6 The stifle and hindleg are outlined.

7 The rear, underneath the tail, is tidied up.

8 The ears are scissored to blend in with the head coat.

9 Special care must be taken when trimming round the eyes.

10 The art of scissoring is to achieve a perfect, rounded shape to the head.

ROUTINE CARE

Teeth should be brushed on a regular basis.

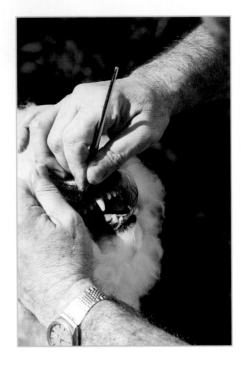

A tooth-scale can be used to remove tartar.

Nails can be trimmed using guillotine-type cutters.

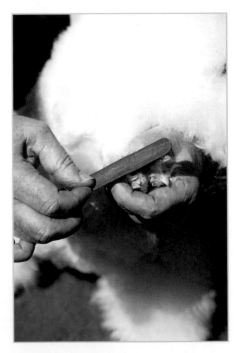

If you prefer, you can use a file on the nails.

Most Bichons learn to enjoy the one-to-one attention that comes from grooming sessions.

FINISHING TOUCHES

- The hair in the Bichon's ears should be plucked regularly. The best time to do this is when the dog is relaxed, curled up on your lap. Take a pair of round-nosed tweezers or use your thumb and forefinger to pluck the hairs, abiding by this general rule: if you can't see it, don't pluck it. Once you've removed the hair that is visible in the ears, then look inside to check for any evidence of mites or infection. If the ears are dirty, red, itchy or foul-smelling, consult your vet.

- Next, turn your attention to your dog's feet. If your Bichon's dewclaws were not removed as a puppy, check them carefully, and trim them if necessary, so that they don't grow and curl around into the foot.

- Check the other nails. Ideally, they should be black, although this makes it more difficult to trim them, as you won't be able to easily see the quick (the nerves and blood supply). Either file the nails down a little, or remove a sliver at a time with guillotine-type clippers. If you are in any doubt about this procedure, ask your veterinarian to supervise your first attempt. It is very important not to cut the quick, as it will bleed, and will be very painful for your dog, making future nail-clipping attempts even more difficult. The back nails rarely need trimming, but, being so light on their feet, a Bichon's front claws do not usually wear down naturally, even if the dog is exercised on a hard surface.

- Staining can be troublesome in a white breed. Tear stains and mouth stains can be removed

Make sure your Bichon has the chance to enjoy life to the full.

by washing the hair in a weak anti-bacterial, non-bleach solution. There are several effective products on the market, although the names vary according to the country you live in. Your breed club will be able to provide you with recommendations.

- Like many small breeds, the Bichon is prone to losing teeth at an early age. Daily tooth-brushing can help to prevent this. Again, get a puppy used to the sensation from an early age, so he is less likely to fight against the procedure when older. Use a toothpaste intended for dogs (they come in tasty meaty flavors), as well as a toothbrush or rubber finger brush (which fits over the tip of a finger). Vets and pet shops usually sell these items.

- When the puppy is teething (at around four to five months of age), his mouth will be particularly sensitive, so be especially gentle with him.

- If you notice anything unusual when grooming your dog, such as a lump, rash or cut, consult your vet.

FAMILY LIFE

The Bichon will quickly become an invaluable member of your family. With its long history as a companion dog, being a good friend and soulmate comes naturally to the Bichon, as you will soon discover.

Caring for the Bichon isn't just about keeping his nails short and his coat tangle-free, it's also about fulfilling the dog's emotional needs. Involving the dog in all family activities is a key part of ensuring his happiness. If he is shut away when visitors come, or is left at home while the family enjoys a weekend stroll, he will feel excluded from his human pack.

This is not to say that the Bichon should never leave your side. This could nurture overdependence, resulting in the dog becoming unable to cope alone—even if left for a few minutes (see Chapter Six). Getting him used to his own company too is important, but you don't have a dog in order to live a separate life from him. If you only want a dog for walks, volunteer at your local rescue shelter!

ADOLESCENT NEEDS

Most Bichons who end up in rescue are there because of a change in their owner's lifestyles (see page 17). But a small number do end up needing a new home thanks to their own actions—and this usually occurs at adolescence. This is the time when owners can really be challenged by their dogs. The adult coat is through, the dog's housebreaking may lapse, and he may begin to challenge your authority, just to see how far he can go. Many Bichons sail through adolescence without a worry, but if yours becomes a little

Adolescence can be a tricky time as your Bichon passes from puppyhood to maturity.

demon, then kind, firm, consistent handling is required during this time—as well as a lot of patience! It is just a phase, and he or she will get through it in the end.

Adolescence is the time when the dog begins to become sexually mature. The temptation can be to neuter the dog or bitch, to put an end to the raging hormones that appear to have turned your doggie angel into a doggie demon. However, neutering is not a "quick fix" behavioral solution. You should neuter for the right reasons—to prevent unwanted puppies being born, and perhaps also because of the health benefits (see below). If you are considering neutering solely because of your dog's behavior—which is not necessarily always effective—then talk to your veterinarian about a "chemical castration," where the effects of neutering can be mimicked, so you can assess whether an operation will be effective.

The decision on when to neuter is controversial. Some breeders and veterinarians believe that you should wait until after 18 months for the male, and, in the bitch, after she has had two seasons. However, others believe that the sooner neutering is carried out, the more significant the health benefits. It is advised that you consult your own veterinary surgeon.

Neutering pros and cons

- If you do not neuter, a dog can be prone to straying, trying to find a bitch. Some dogs are lost forever, or are involved in car accidents. Determined in-season females can also be hell-bent on escaping from the yard, so you must be especially vigilant.

- A bitch in season will be irresistible to other dogs, so should be kept away from them. Although the Bichon can be carried easily, she should still be kept away from public places, as male dogs in the area will quickly pick up her scent. If they can, they will pester you, scrabbling up to get to the dog in your arms.
- There can be some mess involved when a bitch comes in season, although most Bichons keep themselves clean.
- Neutering removes many health risks (such as prostate cancer in dogs and pyometra in bitches) and also reduces the chance of mammary cancer.
- Neutering can result in dogs putting on a little weight, as they are generally slightly less active than their entire counterparts. Monitoring the dog's weight, and adjusting the diet accordingly, soon remedies this.
- Urinary incontinence in spayed bitches can occur, but the risks are generally deemed very small.
- The coat can become thicker in neutered animals.
- Many Bichon enthusiasts say a neutered male is the ideal pet—loving but without "boy" habits (of mounting, leg-cocking, etc.).
- Whether you decide to neuter your Bichon or not, you should discuss the matter with your veterinarian, who will be able to discuss the pros and cons in more depth, and in relation to your particular dog.

VETERAN CARE

The Bichon Frisé is a long-lived breed, with the average dog living to between 12 and 14 years,

Fortunately, Bichons are a long-lived breed.

though many reach their mid- to late teens. The Bichon generally doesn't show signs of aging as early as some other dogs, and is usually sprightly and playful well into double figures. However, having such a good life expectancy does mean that the Bichon is older for longer, so it is important to be aware of how his needs will change as he ages.

- An older dog may slow down a little; he may tire more quickly on walks, or be less agile around the house. He may need help getting up and down stairs, on and off furniture, and in and out of the car.

- The digestion generally slows too, and many dogs do better on three or four small meals a day rather than two feedings.

- Nails may need cutting more frequently, because of the reduced exercise the dog may be getting.

- If a dog is exercising less, he will be burning off fewer calories, so keep a close eye on his weight to ensure your dog does not get plump. Obesity reduces life expectancy and puts pressure on the aging joints and heart—which should be avoided at all costs.

- An elderly Bichon will probably sleep more—ideally on your lap! Many owners have found that a Bichon becomes even more affectionate in old age. Make sure the crate is in a warm, draft-free location, and that his bedding is cozy too—so he has a comfortable "snooze spot" should your lap not be available.

- Make sure that younger dogs (and children) do not pester or over-tire the oldie, and that his crate is a no-go area—somewhere he can rest undisturbed.

- A routine veterinarian visit every six months, instead of yearly, is advisable so any health problems can be treated quickly. Any concerns you have should be reported promptly—for example, a change in drinking or eating habits, incontinence, or any behavioral changes.

BILLY THE (ETERNAL) KID

When Julie Stupart from Bromsgrove, Worcestershire, was looking for a new Bichon to join her family, she was adamant that she didn't want an older dog. Persuaded against her wishes to "road-test" one, she hasn't looked back since.

"When we moved from Edinburgh in Scotland, to Bromsgrove, 10 years ago, we decided to get a dog, as my daughters were so homesick," says Julie. "Nicola was 12 years old, and Michelle was 14, but we needed a breed that didn't cast hair, as Michelle has asthma. We did some research and concluded that the Bichon was the dog for us.

"We contacted a breeder, but she wasn't keen initially, saying that she wouldn't sell a puppy to be a children's pet. We explained that the children were not little ones, and that the dog would be a family dog, and she agreed to consider us. She was very particular about who her dogs went to, and we had to visit a few times, and also attend a grooming lesson.

"When a puppy became available, we took Clyde. Being such a lovely-looking breed, Clyde was a child magnet, and Nicola and Michelle's new friends at school were enthralled with him, and they all wanted to pet him. He certainly helped my daughters to settle in and to overcome their homesickness.

"Sadly, Clyde died of a viral infection when he was just three. We were all heartbroken and went back to the breeder for another puppy. She had a litter at the time, but suggested we look at one of her older dogs—a four-year-old ex–show dog called Billy.

"We were adamant that we wanted a puppy. We viewed the litter, but still the breeder recommended Billy. I wasn't keen at all. I felt that Clyde had been such a character, and that puppies grow up to mold themselves in with the family. In the end, I agreed to take Billy home to just see how we got on. The breeder said we could take him back if it didn't work out, and we could still have a puppy too when the litter was old enough.

"We took Billy home, and I just thought, 'What have

To begin with, Julie wasn't sure about taking on four-year-old Billy.

we done?' This wasn't helped by the fact that he howled all night. I called the breeder the next day, and explained that it just wasn't working out—that Billy was obviously missing his family. The breeder asked where he had slept, and I explained that we had bought him a nice, big bed, which we had put in our large kitchen, leaving the door open so he had access to the hall. She suggested we put him in his traveling box, with fleece bedding inside, keep the box door open, and shut the kitchen door. It worked a treat! We had just given Billy too much open space, when, in fact, he wanted a small, cozy environment at bedtime. That night, he slept like a log!

"Billy had been one of several much-loved dogs at the breeder's house, but he thrived being an only dog—getting 100 percent single attention and love. We coaxed him upstairs, where he hadn't been allowed before, and he slowly got used to sleeping on our beds! We quickly got used to his little idiosyncrasies too.

"When Charlie, the puppy, came along, Billy was like a doting father. If the pup whimpered, Billy would go and lie beside him and lick him. He has always been top dog, although Charlie does challenge him sometimes, especially as Billy is 10 years old now.

"If you didn't know Billy's age, you would never suspect he was an older dog. We have noticed some changes that have slowly crept in, but that's only because we have known him for so long that we can see the differences. For example, he's not as fit as he once was. He can't jump up on things as he used to; one time, he couldn't quite make the jump and hurt his back as he fell back down. Now, he will stand in front of whatever he wants to jump on to and will look at us, as if to say, 'Come on, lift me up!'

"When we walk the dogs now, Billy sometimes lags behind a little, whereas Charlie is chugging away at the front and bouncing around like a spring lamb. Billy's much more fussy too—if it's raining outside, and we're going out for a walk, you can see he's not impressed. He much prefers to stay inside where it's warm and dry.

"Billy's play sessions with Charlie are shorter too. Billy will only take a certain amount of ankle-nipping before he tells Charlie he's had enough!

"I can see now that Billy was just what we needed. The breeder was right. Being such a quiet, loving dog, he really helped us through the grieving process. We were all feeling so empty after Clyde, who was such an outgoing, mischievous dog. Having Billy, who was well behaved, mature, and so gentle and affectionate, helped us a great deal, and we quickly fell in love with him. The breeder knew all along that we would never take him back! He's one of the best things that has ever happened to us."

Billy (right) quickly became like a doting father to puppy Charlie (left).

EUTHANASIA

Although they are long-lived, sadly the Bichon doesn't live forever, and the time will eventually come when you have to say good-bye. Having to part with a loving, loyal companion is incredibly difficult. However, it is every owner's duty to ensure that their pet does not suffer and is allowed to die peacefully and with dignity.

If your Bichon is in pain, and can no longer be helped, your veterinarian will discuss euthanasia with you. Often, it is called "putting the dog to sleep"—with good reason; the injection puts the animal into a peaceful, deep sleep and he gently passes away.

It is advisable to have already considered what to do with the body, as making such a decision while coping with the emotional loss can be bewildering. There are various options, such as taking the body home with you to bury in the yard (subject to local laws); having him individually cremated and keeping or scattering the ashes; or burying him in a pet cemetery. Alternatively, if you prefer to take only your memories home with you, your veterinarian can dispose of the body.

Dealing with the loss of a pet can be very hard. If you need extra support to cope, ask your veterinarian for details of a pet bereavement counseling service. The Internet has many sites dedicated to this subject, with owners all over the world sharing their experiences and helping others in a similar situation. A popular site, which might help you, is www.petloss.com.

SUNSET FOR SUNNY

Losing any pet is difficult, but when you are responsible for bringing a dog into the world, it is particularly hard to see him leave it, as Maureen Miles from Harrow Weald, Middlesex, knows only too well.

"Sunny (Ch. Alareen Precious Sundancer) was in the first litter I bred," explains Maureen. "There were four pups, and I kept two, Sunny and his brother. You could tell they both had show quality—they really stood out by eight weeks of age. Sunny went on to outperform his brother, though, as he was such a showman in the ring, and he became our first Champion. And he kept on winning, becoming an Irish Champion as

well. One of the highlights was in 1993, when he won Best of Breed at Crufts, and then came in third in the Toy group. I was so proud of him that day—and every day!

"Sunny was a great member of the family. He was bubbly and affectionate, gentle, excellent with children, and very, very lovable.

"He was always very healthy, but one day, when he was $11\frac{1}{2}$ years old, he was going up the step by the back door, and suddenly went lame in one leg. His cruciate ligament had gone. He had an operation, and the veterinarian was sure that Sunny would recover, but time went on and on, and he still couldn't put weight on the leg. The vet couldn't understand why it wasn't healing.

Sunny: Still much missed.

"Then, Sunny's other back leg suddenly went. It was the other cruciate. Now, he couldn't stand at all, and we knew he wouldn't get better. He couldn't go to the toilet by himself, and he had to be carried everywhere. For such a previously bouncy dog, it was a terrible life and we couldn't put him through it.

"Having Sunny put to sleep was one of the worst things I have ever had to do. I brought him into the world, so I was especially close to him, but you owe it to your dog not to let him suffer. From puppyhood, they give you love and affection, without asking anything in return. Making sure they don't suffer pain is the owner's duty.

"I grieved for a long time after losing Sunny. It's now 18 months on since he died and I still miss him.

"Since Sunny, I have also lost two-year-old Grace, who was a week away from having a litter of puppies. She was perfectly healthy, and then suddenly died—together with her unborn pups. The post-mortem revealed that the pups were oversized and had cut off Grace's blood supply to her heart.

"She was a lovely, happy, beautiful dog, and it was tragic to lose her so young. But whatever age they die, whether it's at two or 22, you still mourn them."

MEMORIES OF MIKO

In 1986, Nanette Catarinella from Pittsburgh, Pennsylvania, got herself a little female Bichon puppy called Miko. Nanette and Miko shared 17 happy years together before Miko became ill and Nanette had to make one of the hardest decisions of her life—to have Miko put to sleep. Here, Nanette describes some of the happier times she shared with Miko and how she came to make that heart-wrenching decision.

"I lived in Dallas, Texas, in 1986 when a co-worker invited me to a party at her house. It was there that I first saw her adorable, fluffy white dog. I thought it was an unclipped Poodle, but I was told that it was actually a Bichon Frisé. Until that day I had never heard of the breed!

"I was immediately drawn to the dog's sweet disposition and bright, intelligent eyes. I already had two cats at home, but I knew that I wanted this dog. I remember telling my husband about the dog that evening and trying to convince him that we needed another pet. He was not interested.

BABY SADNESS
"Shortly after that time, we learned that I would not be able to have children. To console me, my husband finally agreed to buy me a Bichon. I checked the newspaper ads and found a local breeder. We made an appointment for the next afternoon. When we arrived at the breeder's home we were greeted by at least a dozen Bichons of varying sizes, from small puppies to adults. They were everywhere!

FALLING IN LOVE
"We were drawn to a lively little pup that came directly to me and curled up in my lap. The breeder tried to steer us to another dog, pointing out that this pup had an obvious underbite, but that didn't matter to me—I wanted a pet, not a show dog, and I was already in love with her.

"Since the puppy was only four weeks old at the time, we had to wait another four weeks until she could be released for adoption. In the meantime, I called my family back in Pittsburgh to tell them that we were getting a new puppy. I asked my three-year-old niece, Crystal, if she could think of a good name for the new puppy. Crystal immediately said, 'You should call her Miko.'

"I thought it was a really cute name and I loved it. 'How did you think of that?' I asked. Crystal replied, 'Mommy just bought me two new dolls. One is Tropical Barbie and the other is her friend, Tropical Miko.' And so our new Bichon was named Miko.

MAKING FRIENDS
"We moved from Dallas to New York City when Miko was a year old. It was a big adjustment to go from a house with a yard to a high-rise apartment in Manhattan. We had to walk the dog several times daily, which proved to be a wonderful way to meet other 'dog' people in the neighborhood.

"We had heard stories about how unfriendly New Yorkers were, but, with Miko, we found that we had an instant conversation starter. She was so friendly and outgoing that everyone wanted to stop and pet her, and she thoroughly enjoyed the attention.

"One weekend, I decided to fly to Pittsburgh to visit my family. I intended to have Miko fly in her carrier under the seat in the airplane cabin. When I was checking in at the gate, the attendant informed me that Miko could not fly in the cabin, but would have to travel in the

"I am the pilot for this flight, and I am also a dog lover..."

baggage compartment. It was a hot summer day and I was concerned with the conditions in the baggage area. I began arguing with the attendant, to the point that I was in tears. Just then, a man in uniform came up to me and asked what the problem was.

"I told him that the airline was insisting that I put my dog in the baggage area and I was afraid for her health. He took one look at Miko's sweet face and said, 'My dear, I am the pilot for this flight and I am also a dog lover. I wouldn't let my dog fly in baggage and neither shall yours. She can fly in the cockpit with me!' And she did just that!

TRAUMATIC TIME
"I moved back to my hometown of Pittsburgh from New York City 10 months later, and my husband and I divorced the following year. My husband got the two cats in the divorce. I kept Miko. The day that my husband moved out of the house was very traumatic for Miko. With the two cats gone, it was the first time that Miko was all alone in the house.

Continued overleaf

Miko: The light of Nanette's life.

Miko: A loving companion for 17 years.

"When I returned home that evening, I found that she had eliminated right in the middle of my bed. It was her way of letting me know that she was upset with me. I decided that Miko needed some company. The next morning I went to the local animal shelter and picked out an adorable little kitten that I named Trinket. The two became inseparable buddies and Miko never had another incident on the bed.

"I eventually remarried, and my new husband, David, is also an animal lover. We decided to add another Bichon to our family two years ago. Adding Phoebe to our household seemed to bring new life to our ageing Miko. She had started to withdraw and do nothing but sleep and eat, but, when Phoebe arrived, she became more active and curious. It was as if she had a new lease on life.

> **66 It was during the last year of Miko's life that old age finally caught up with her. 99**

SIGNS OF AGE

"Miko lived a long and happy life. She never suffered from any illness and was never on any medication. She did develop cataracts and had some hearing loss, but that was only to be expected in an ageing dog.

"It was during the last year of Miko's life that old age finally caught up with her and she began slowly to deteriorate. She no longer wanted to be held and she became confused and fearful. Although she continued to eat, she was losing weight. I eventually had to confine her to the kitchen after she suffered several falls down the steps.

"The last six months were emotionally draining. I knew the time had come to say good-bye, but I just couldn't bring myself to end her life. I kept hoping that Miko would go naturally, but the poor dear was hanging on. It became evident that the quality of her life was diminished and I had to help her let go.

FINAL DECISION

"I finally called our veterinarian and made an appointment to have Miko evaluated. I wanted a professional to be the one to make the final decision although, in my heart, I already knew what that would be. I asked if he recommended that I be there with her to the end.

"He explained that it was a personal decision and that even he could not stay when his own

dog was put to sleep. He described how he would give her a sedative prior to administering a lethal injection that would gently end her life.

TIME TO LET GO

"I asked if we could give Miko the sedative before bringing her in, as she no longer enjoyed riding in the car and traveling in the carrier made her agitated. The veterinarian agreed that it would be less stressful for Miko that way.

"The morning of the appointment, my husband gave her the pill. Within an hour, she began to relax and I was able to hold her comfortably as I said my tearful good-byes. I was so distraught that my husband offered to take her alone, and I reluctantly agreed. I did feel guilty for not staying with her, but I could not bring myself to go along. That was the most difficult part of the decision, and one that I am still struggling with.

WONDERFUL MEMORIES

"I have such wonderful memories of my dear little Miko. She was a loving companion for 17 years, and the one constant in my life—through several relocations, a divorce and remarriage. I have her ashes in a tasteful wooden box with her name on it, and I keep several photos around to remind me of our life together."

CHAPTER SIX

BROADENING HORIZONS

Photo by www.actionshots.me.uk/

The Bichon is frequently described as a large dog in a small body. Although he was bred largely for companionship, his intelligence and athleticism should not be underestimated. Playful in nature, taking a lively interest in all that is going on around him, the Bichon is a breed that will thrive if his basic training is extended.

CANINE GOOD CITIZEN

The Canine Good Citizen Dog Scheme run by the UK Kennel Club and the Good Citizen Program run by the American Kennel Club are excellent places to begin if you want to take your Bichon's training a step further. Both programs have the same objectives: to encourage responsible dog ownership and to educate dog owners about the benefits of having a well-behaved pet.

The programs test the dog's ability to behave in a calm, controlled and confident manner in a variety of situations, including the following:

- Walking on a loose lead in a controlled manner
- Being approached and petted by a stranger
- Getting in and out of a car safely
- Meeting another dog
- Being groomed and handled
- Responding to a number of basic commands (such as Sit, Down, etc.).

In America, the AKC runs a two-part program, at the end of which the dog must pass an examination made up of 10 tests that cover basic behavior and control. In the UK, there are grades—Puppy Foundation, Bronze, Silver and Gold—with the pass criteria becoming steadily harder as the dog progresses.

Many training clubs now offer Good Citizen schemes as part of their training programs, and in most cases, it is relatively easy to join a club fairly close to your home. If you are interested in finding out more, your national kennel club will be able to provide you with details of clubs in your area.

CITIZEN DINO

Julia Marsden, of Birmingham, West Midlands, and her Bichon, Simway Sir Dino, began training for the Canine Good Citizen Scheme in 2003. Here, Julia describes the training involved and why she thinks the scheme is so valuable.

"I first discovered the Canine Good Citizen Scheme at an Obedience show I was attending with my other Bichon, Bobby. Back then, there was only one test, rather than the Puppy Foundation, Bronze, Silver and Gold awards there are today. I decided to take the test, which involved some very basic obedience exercises and answering some questions about dog ownership, and we passed. I felt it had been a useful experience, and I decided I would put Dino through his paces as well.

"I was already a member of a dog training club, but they did not run the scheme when I began training my dogs. However, when they launched their Canine Good Citizen scheme, I enrolled Dino immediately.

NEW SKILLS
"The training is fun and it is up to each individual how far they want to take it. The Bronze award is quite basic, involving carrying a poop-scoop, making sure your dog is wearing the correct identification, being able to put on the dog's collar and lead correctly, walking the dog on a lead without him pulling, and so on.

"At the other end of the grade, the Gold award is more intensive. For example, you have to perform a recall while walking, the dog has to walk at your side without being on a lead, and the dog must remain in a Down-stay for two minutes— 30 seconds of which must be with you out of sight. You also have to get the dog to stop where he is while he is loose, he must obey you when you send him to his bed, and he must leave any food offered to him until you give him permission to take it.

"I found the Gold the most difficult level to pass with Dino. I remember training for the send-away. We used a mat for this exercise—the dog had to go to the mat and remain there until he was called back. To encourage this, we gave treats to the dog once they got on the mat and sat. One evening at training classes, our instructor, Gary, was getting us to practice walking the dog to heel off-lead while he set up the send-away mat. He put the mat on the floor with a jar of treats placed behind it. The idea was that, while the class was practicing heel work, he would call us over one at a time to practice the send-away. Dino, however, had other ideas!

TEMPTING TREATS
"As soon as Gary put down the treats next to the mat, Dino ran straight over to the mat and sat down, expecting to get a treat for his efforts. I retrieved him and tried to carry on with heel work, but Dino just kept running back to the mat every time I let go of him. Finally realizing that just sitting on the mat wasn't going to earn him a treat, Dino picked up the treat jar and brought it back to me! In the end, he mastered both his send-away and his heel work, but that evening was quite a session!

"I'd recommend the scheme to anyone. It teaches people how to be responsible dog owners, and all the tasks the dogs have to complete successfully are things that your dog should be able to cope with in normal, day-to-day life. The benefits are obvious—knowing you can take your dog out without any situation becoming out of control. Most importantly, being able to stop your dog in his tracks, even at a distance, is a lifesaver. Imagine if he was heading in a beeline towards a busy road!

"Dino took to training extremely well. I think the use of treats had something to do with it! Dino is pretty typical of a Bichon, and they can be stubborn at times, but this is why it is important to use positive, motivational training. Bichons are highly intelligent, and as long as you try to gain their cooperation rather than force them to do something, they can learn a wide range of things very quickly.

"My advice would be to find a really good training club and start the scheme by going to classes. After that, who knows? You may well decide, as I have done, that you and your Bichon enjoyed the experience so much that you want to go on to more advanced training."

Dino with his Bronze, Silver, and Gold Good Citizen awards.

COMPETITIVE OBEDIENCE

If your Bichon enjoyed his basic training, there is every chance that he will be ready to try some more challenging exercises.

The Bichon may not seem an obvious breed choice for Obedience, but there is no doubt that he can acquit himself very well in this sport, and there is the added advantage of having an extremely well-trained dog that is a pleasure to take anywhere.

Although Bichons are highly intelligent, they can also become bored quite easily, so it is vital to make training as fun as possible. Bichons respond far better to short bursts of training (approximately 10–15 minutes per session only) with lots of praise, treats and games, than they do to rigorous, long sessions where they are compelled to do something for fear of punishment.

Equally important is motivation. Find out what really gets your Bichon going. Often it is food, but it could equally be a game with a favorite toy. If your Bichon feels that he will receive something at the end of a training session that will make all his effort worthwhile, you will find he is a lot more eager to please.

Ron and Jacqui McKenzie from Bury-St.-Edmunds, Suffolk, have been involved in Obedience since the 1970s, first with crossbreeds, and later with Bichons—indeed, their mutual love of the sport was responsible for their meeting and marrying! Here, Ron recounts their experiences. . . .

"I got into Obedience when I adopted a stray puppy and decided to take him to training classes. He did so well that my trainer suggested I go on to competition training classes, and it was there that Jacqui and I first met.

"Our first purebred Obedience dogs were Border Collies. However, Jacqui's last Collie proved to be very large and boisterous, and we decided that we would like a smaller breed. We were competing at a show when we noticed that the ring adjacent to ours contained small, white, fluffy little dogs that we rather liked the look of. Jacqui went over to have a chat with one of the handlers, Chris Wyatt, and said she would like a Bichon. Then, a year later at the same show, Chris came over and said, 'I have got something for you,' and with that, she presented us with a 12-week-old Bichon puppy. We were hooked!

"We have now trained six Bichons. They are very intelligent little dogs and take to Obedience training easily. Our dogs took first, third and sixth places in the novice class at a Toy Dog Limited show last spring, and first and third in our club's novice progress test. In Open shows, Border Collies and German Shepherd dogs tend to steal most of the prizes, but our Bichons certainly do not disgrace us—they usually finish somewhere in

Above: Jamie presents the dumb-bell.

Left: Attentive heelwork performed off-lead.

the middle of the class, and we live in hope for the day when they take first place.

"Jacqui's Bichon, Jamie (Jaunty James of High Trees), does one of the fastest retrieves in the business for his size, and it is quite a sight to see him perform in a hall with a slippery floor when he grabs the dumbbell and slides to a standstill before returning!

"I would recommend Obedience to anyone with a Bichon, but I think it's important to remember that you are in it mainly for the fun. Bichons *can* do extremely well, and the judges certainly seem to appreciate a change from the usual Collies or German Shepherds, but Bichons do tend not to produce the close, 'wraparound' heel work that judges expect.

"However, quite aside from the winning side to competitions, there's the added benefit of having a well-trained dog. I was particularly proud of Sadie (Saucy Sadie) at a Bichon Club party. During the interval about 20–25 dogs were running loose—it was really quite hectic! Among all that distraction, I called Sadie to me and she immediately ran out from the pack and sat to heel.

"If anyone reading this is thinking of taking up Obedience, I would recommend that they concentrate on standard training first, and then go along to a few competitions. Talk to the handlers, who are always very friendly and more than happy to help, and ask them for advice on where to go for more advanced training. Don't overwork your dog, though. First and foremost, you should enjoy your Bichon, and remember that play and treats do more for a Bichon's concentration than boring and endless training regimens."

Above: The Sit-stay exercise.

Left: Sadie finding the correct scent cloth.

AGILITY

Agility is a kind of obstacle course for dogs. Dogs must complete the course as quickly and as accurately as possible. The obstacles include the following:

- Hurdles
- A long or broad jump
- Tunnels and chutes
- Poles, which the dog must weave through
- A seesaw or teeter board
- A dog walk (a narrow, elevated walkway with a ramp at either end)
- An A-frame (a steep, A-shaped ramp)

For small dogs, there is "mini-Agility," and Bichons have excelled themselves in this. Their quick intelligence and love of fun makes them ideal candidates. However, because Agility is a demanding sport, puppies and growing dogs are not allowed to compete in case they damage their delicate joints and ligaments.

Most kennel clubs impose an age limit of between 12 and 18 months before a dog is permitted to enter Agility competitions. Even more important, remember that no dog under this age should be encouraged to jump, even at home, and no matter how much they seem to enjoy it.

Once your Bichon is old enough to try Agility, you need to make sure that he is fit enough—and that goes for you too! Being bred as a lapdog, the average Bichon does not need a great deal of exercise, but you should make sure that your Bichon is getting a sensible amount if he is going to be able to take part in Agility.

It is strongly advised that you join an Agility club if you are interested in taking up this sport. Your national kennel club will provide you with details.

PEEKA PROVES THEM WRONG!

Michele Wells from Sammamish, Washington, has been involved in Agility for the last three years, and proves that Bichons can bomb around an agility course with the best of them—even Peeka, who has a slight physical disability.

"I first saw Agility on television and became enthralled by it, but it wasn't until I got my first Bichon, Peeka, that I started to get involved. Before Peeka, I had kept Poodles, but I 'discovered' Bichons through my in-laws. I fell in love with the breed—they have so much personality and they are very smart.

"Peeka has a stiff back leg that she can't bend, so she doesn't seem an obvious candidate for Agility. However, when she was about six months old, she jumped the baby gate in the kitchen from a standstill. She also ran laps of the backyard at full speed. We have a tree stump at the end of our yard and she would run long laps around that, using the stump to bank her turns. Her stiff leg did not seem to slow her at all—she was incredibly fast!

Peeka flies over the hurdle.

"After seeing her in action, I decided I needed to do something with Peeka to keep her active and busy. I wanted to build a strong relationship between us and to keep her mentally challenged. I also had a feeling that, because Peeka was so smart, if I didn't find a way of keeping her amused, her behavior might not turn out to be all that I and my family wanted.

"Having made the decision to get involved in Agility, it was really easy to take the next positive step. I started out by doing a little research on the Internet and checking out the clubs in the local telephone directory. I settled on the Seattle Agility Center, which ran classes for puppies. I signed up for just one cycle of classes, figuring that I could quit at any time if Peeka or I didn't like it, but we took to it straight away. It's a wonderful club— everyone was very kind and relaxed.

"Our initial training involved handler techniques and learning to work as a team in our classes with other dogs and their owners. Then we moved on to learning commands, to help the dogs execute the obstacles. Peeka was very quick to learn, but each dog learns at his own pace. Some people attend no more than a class a week, while others can become so involved that they practice regularly outside of class, attend special workshops, subscribe to chat rooms and so on.

"Peeka has a disability, so I limit her training, as I don't want her to overdo things. I'm sure she would do more if I let her. When I tell her we're off to training class, she becomes really excited. If I deviate from my normal route when we travel there, she looks at me with real concern! In class, she really gives it her all. Occasionally, she can get a little sidetracked because she wants to say hello to everyone. For example,

Continued overleaf

"Peeka was really keen to compete—even if I was not!"

we have to say hello to the instructor properly before we begin training, or she will run off course to do that.

"I'll never forget when we made the decision to compete—Peeka was ready before I was! I had been thinking about competing but was very nervous about the idea, so my husband, my son and I attended a trial hosted by my agility club, to get an idea of what it was all about. We sat in the stands and watched the other dogs compete. Peeka had a terrible time! She was crying and trying to pull us on to the course—she desperately wanted to compete. She was ready even if I was not!

"Due to Peeka's back leg, I doubt that we will achieve any titles in Agility, but that doesn't really matter to us; we just enjoy the taking part. My proudest moments are when Peeka performs a clean run with no faults within the course time. This is no easy feat for any Agility dog, let alone one with a disability! I love it when she shows the spectators that she can do it, even though one of her legs does not work properly.

"I have another Bichon now, Stanley. He also loves Agility training. He is not even a year old yet,

but we are already in our second round of classes and he is performing beautifully. He is much faster than Peeka, which means that we have to train slightly differently and I need to run faster, too. I have even started working out! The sky's the limit with Stanley. If he performs as well as I think he's going to, I believe we'll earn titles.

"I would advise anyone interested in Agility to have a go. It's great fun. You should make sure that you're doing it for your dog, though. It should be play, not work, and your dog will need kind, positive instruction in order to build the trust and obedience needed to be successful. Find a club that matches your own attitude and lifestyle, and above all, expect the unexpected—you *never* know what's going to happen at an Agility class or competition!"

Michele with Peeka (left), and her new star, Stanley.

STARRING SACHA

Breeder Ally Marquiss of Moreton, Wirral, is the proud owner of five Bichons, ranging in age from 11 months to 13 years. She is a firm believer that an active Bichon is a happy Bichon.

"When I was on holiday in Gran Canaria, I wanted to send a postcard home. The one I ended up buying had two adult Bichons with a puppy on the front, and that started me off. When I got home, I started to look around for a Bichon, and eventually managed to get Chester at six months of age.

"I first discovered Agility when I owned a crossbreed called Jenna. We thoroughly enjoyed ourselves, but it wasn't until I got Chester (now 13) that I took up Agility seriously. When Chester was about a year old, my local training club started a new Agility section, and I jumped at the chance to join.

"Fortunately, Chester was already quite well trained—dogs need to have the basics mastered before they have a go at something like Agility. The fact that we had done some Competitive Obedience training was also a help. Chester picked it up really quickly and seemed to thoroughly enjoy himself. Since then, I have taken all my dogs to Agility classes.

"A happy Bichon should be confident, outgoing and full of fun—a dog with 'attitude' is ideal for Agility. That said, I also believe that a shy, nervous Bichon can benefit enormously from Agility training. It helps to restore confidence and a sense of fun, and for me, Agility is all about having fun with your dog.

"I am currently training Sacha (nine) and Chaos (three). We train about once a week. It's a bit of a handful trying to train two dogs at once, but we manage. Usually, I train one dog on a certain set of equipment (the hurdles, for example), get my

Chester flies through the tire.

breath back while our classmates have a go, and then train on the same equipment with the other dog. It works amazingly well, although the attention, praise and liver treats also help!

"Sacha is my star dog at the moment—although I love them all dearly. In July 2002, she won the Starter class at a competition. She ran a fantastic, lovely clear round. It was a really proud moment for us. After that, we moved up to the next level.

"Sacha frequently amazes people at Agility competitions. I also breed and show dogs, so Sacha can often be seen running the course in full show coat, and it's quite a sight! She loves it so much—you can see it. With her fluffy, white coat she looks really quite beautiful. The downside of this, of course, is that if we've been

Continued overleaf

66 If your dog does something wrong, you haven't made your instructions clear. 99

training or competing on a wet, windy day, there's an awful lot of work to do to get her coat clean again when we get home!

"Sacha runs the course very fast. So fast, in fact, that I have slipped over more times than I care to remember. The best purchase I have ever made is a pair of Astroturf shoes, so that I don't fall over quite so often.

"All my Bichons really enjoy themselves at Agility, and I would recommend it to anyone.

However, you need to remember that it's all about having fun. Don't take it too seriously or you can lose sight of that.

"You should remember that if your dog does something wrong, it's because you haven't made your instructions clear enough. Don't scold the dog for your own mistakes. With Bichons, you need to be positive. Use lots of praise and treats, and always, always end your training on a good note."

Chaos: At the start of his Agility career.

Sacha: A serious competitor, taking on all the mini breeds.

FLYBALL

Flyball is a relay race for dogs. In most cases, two competing teams, each containing four dogs, race against each other. A dog is released from the starting line, and has to run to the other end of the track, jumping over four hurdles on the way. At the end of the track is a Flyball box, which the dog must trigger to release a tennis ball. The dog catches the ball and then races back over the four hurdles to the starting line. As soon as the dog crosses the line, the second dog is released, and so on. The winning team is the one in which all four dogs have successfully completed their run in the fastest time.

Flyball is relatively easy to learn and it is enormous fun for dogs and people alike. It is, however, highly competitive, and it requires dogs and their handlers to be able to work well as part of a team. If this sounds like you and your Bichon, why not give it a go?

Your national kennel club will be able to let you know about clubs in your area, and with flyball becoming an increasingly popular canine sport, the number of clubs is growing all the time.

SPEEDIE BY NAME...

Lynn Speedie of Monkton, Maryland, is the proud owner of two Bichons—four-year-old Poppy (CGC, Therapy Dog, FD, FDX, FDCh, FM) and three-year old Prince Ari.

"I first discovered Bichons when my 80-year-old mother came to live with me, bringing her little white dog, Muffin. Muffin 'found' Mom, so no one really knew what breed she was for sure, but most people seemed to think she was a Bichon. Muffin was the sweetest dog I have ever known, and I have always loved Bichons ever since.

"When I got Poppy, I took her along to pet training courses. We felt a bit lost when we finished the course, so our trainer, who knew about Flyball, suggested I might like to try it. She recommended the Jet Set club in Bainbridge Pennsylvania, which we now belong to.

"In my area, there are few teams, so Poppy and I have to commute an hour and a half each way to training, but it is well worth it. We were very lucky to find Jet Set. Their philosophy is that, while everyone wants to win and have a fast dog, it is more important that our dogs have fun—which is just what we do!

"It took Poppy about six months to learn all of the elements in Flyball. We went to weekly lessons and practiced at home as much as we could—about 10–15 minutes once or twice a day. Poppy picked it up really quickly. Jet Set follows a positive training method—the dogs are never scolded—and there is a lot of 'back-chaining' (where training is broken down into elements that are learned separately and then put together into a sequence).

"We began with low jumps, then regular jumps, then jumps in a line. Poppy worked on

Continued overleaf

" My happy little dog disappeared, and I felt terrible for her. "

Poppy: A keen Flyball competitor.

a mock box that she learned to jump on and take a ball stuck to the top of it. At home, we worked on retrieving a stationary ball, then bringing the ball back over the jumps. Then we began on the real box, which makes a bang when the dog hits it and triggers the ball. Poppy did not like the loud noise to begin with, but she gradually got used to it for extremely tasty treats! Finding something that motivates your dog is half the battle.

"Once Poppy had mastered the jumps and retrieving the ball, we moved on to passing another dog at the starting gate, then running and passing with another team running in the next lane. Before we knew it, we were playing proper Flyball!

"After about a year of running tournaments with Poppy, we hit a problem. A dog from the opposing team ran across into Poppy's lane and started chasing her. Unfortunately, this happened several times in succeeding tournaments, and eventually, Poppy refused to run. My happy little dog disappeared and I felt terrible for her. I thought long and hard about continuing in Flyball, but I finally decided that, because Poppy really loved the game, we would continue to try.

BRAVING THE COURSE
"It took nine months of retraining, and a lot of steak—Poppy needed an excellent incentive to brave the course. To make things more difficult, we had to retrain at tournaments, because it was only in tournaments, with other dogs running alongside, that Poppy was afraid. Fortunately, the judges were very sympathetic and tried to allow

us as much time as they could. A heat at a time, we made our comeback. My proudest moment was when she achieved her Flyball Master title and the whole building exploded with applause. What a moment!

"Poppy adores Flyball. She loves her doggie and human team-mates and she is so happy to see them all. Of course, I think Poppy is very special—a once-in-a-lifetime dog—but I think that many Bichons could play Flyball and really love it. Whenever we can, Poppy and I go to 'Bichon Bashes' where we demonstrate Flyball in the hope of encouraging people to have a go.

BAD TREATMENT
"Some of the dogs in our club have behavioral issues or are simply bored. My other Bichon, Prince Ari, is a rescued Bichon who was chained up all day, and, judging from his reaction to people when I first got him, he was badly mistreated. To begin with, he would hardly let anyone go near him. He still has a way to go before he becomes a totally happy and well-adjusted dog, but he has improved enormously.

"I believe that Flyball, and the kindness that our teammates showed to Prince Ari, is partly responsible for that. He has already learned to go over a jump and get a ball. Flyball is really boosting his confidence and now he looks for treats from people and even gets up on their laps!

Lynn and Poppy: A winning team.

Photo by Lisa T. Silhan, Paw Prints Professional Pet Photography

"The social element in Flyball is also very special—it is such fun to be with other people who love their dogs as much as you do. No one should be put off by the occasional disparaging remarks people may make about the fact that you are running with a lapdog. Bichons are intelligent, enthusiastic and very athletic. Their love of life and of everything in it will enrich and delight any team. I think Poppy has more than demonstrated that."

THERAPY WORK

As the owner of a Bichon, you will be well aware of the joys of dog ownership—the cuddles, the unconditional love, the playful times and the walks. Interaction with pets has scientifically proven benefits, such as lowering stress and blood pressure, relieving anxiety and boosting the immune system. Imagine how empty your life would suddenly seem if your dog were no longer there. Sadly, this is the case for many people, such as the elderly forced to move to a nursing home.

Fortunately, there is a small army of volunteers trying to help animal lovers who are no longer able to own their own dogs. Therapy dog programs have gained an increasingly high profile in latter years, as the benefits associated with them have hit the headlines. All the dogs in question have to pass character tests and prove themselves totally trustworthy before they are allowed to belong to a recognized therapy organization.

If you have a laid-back dog with an extremely affectionate nature—which applies to lots and lots of Bichons—he could make an ideal therapy dog. Not only will your dog love the work, but you will derive enormous satisfaction from the amount of good you are doing for others less fortunate than yourself. If this type of work appeals to you, your national kennel club will be able to provide you with the details of the main therapy dog organizations in your country.

BICHON BENEFITS

Gillian Johnson, from Hilton, Derbyshire, has been a therapy dog volunteer for more than 15 years. Beginning with her German Shepherd, Gillian now continues her good work with her two Bichons, Virginia (12) and Clarence (9).

"I became interested in therapy work because of a friend of mine, Madeleine Pickup, who had been involved with the Pets As Therapy (PAT) scheme since its inception. At that time, I owned a German Shepherd dog, Ricky. As Ricky had a beautiful temperament, Madeleine suggested that I might like to put him forward for therapy work.

"I got my first Bichon, Virginia, somewhat indirectly. She was bred to be a show dog, but a slipped kneecap cut short her show career and so she was rehomed as a pet with my mother-in-law. When my mother-in-law was no longer able to keep her, she came to my husband and me.

"Being our first Bichon, Virginia was a constant surprise and delight to us. We were amazed at just how tough she was! Not long after we got her, we went on holiday to the Lake District, and Virginia thought nothing of walking 10 miles every day. Although Bichons look very glamorous in the show ring, they are very uncomplicated dogs underneath—they love to roam around the fields like any other dog!

"Since Ricky, I have registered both of my Bichons as therapy dogs, Clarence being the latest. At first, I found it quite difficult to find somewhere to visit, and I approached several places before I found somewhere willing to take us. We are now once-a-fortnight visitors at a local residential home for the elderly, Horace Pritchard House.

FUNNY STORIES

"Clarence and Virginia are certainly coversation starters. The staff at the home tell us that, after we leave, the residents talk about the dogs for hours. I have also noticed that residents who have had to leave their beloved pets behind when they moved into the home are encouraged to talk about their own pets and they recount funny stories and memories. Perhaps the most rewarding aspect, though, is the effect the dogs have on residents who suffer from dementia.

"The staff encourage the residents to stroke the dogs and, as a result, we see a smile, or even a few words—often a major breakthrough! One particular lady, who had very advanced dementia and was totally unable to communicate, would sit for hours talking to the dog, making complete sense all the time!

"For the dogs' part, they love the visits to the home, especially as they are given treats by the staff and residents. I think they revel in all the attention they get. Virginia seems to particularly love the men. She does a special little dance for them and she is a real flirt!

"If you have the right dog, and would like to get involved with therapy work, it is important to make sure that you can live up to your commitments.

Clarence: A dog can break the ice and be a real conversation-starter.

BEING MISSED

"It's no good starting off with the best intentions and then starting to miss visits because you really don't have the time. Residents *will* notice if you have missed a visit, and they feel let down by it. On the few occasions I have had to forgo a visit, I'm always asked on the following visit why I haven't been!

"It's also important to make sure the dogs are enjoying themselves. Most dogs with the right temperament will love the work, but I try to ensure that Clarence and Virginia never work for more than 45 minutes, because they can become tired after that."

CHAPTER SEVEN

SEEKING PERFECTION

Showing is one of the oldest canine disciplines and can be great fun—you will get to meet lots of other people who love their Bichons as much as you, you will see an awful lot of dogs, and, you may even win a few competitions.

However, showing can also be extremely hard work. The cost of traveling around the country, with dogs and equipment in tow, can be considerable. Competition is fierce, and if you are to stand any chance of success, you will need to spend a lot of time making sure that your Bichon is in tip-top condition.

SHOW QUALITY

In the first instance, you need an experienced breeder or exhibitor to give an honest evaluation of your Bichon. There is no point in getting involved in showing unless you have a dog that is likely to make the grade.

In most cases, the best plan is to buy a puppy with show potential (see page 24) and keep your fingers crossed that he will blossom into a top-quality animal. You should remember, though, that there are no guarantees.

BREED STANDARD

In the show ring, each breed is judged against its Breed Standard. This is a written blueprint, giving a picture of what the "perfect" dog should look like. The dog who wins his class will be the one who, in the judge's opinion, conforms most closely to the Breed Standard.

Breed Standards differ slightly between countries, but the following explains the key points of the UK and US Standards. For a full, official Breed Standard, contact your national kennel club.

General appearance

The Bichon has a smart, white, powder-puff coat of loose curls. He has a jolly personality, as seen by the tail being carried gaily over his back, and he is well balanced, with no exaggeration.

The head framed by stunning white coat, and the dark, lustrous eyes, are among the most important breed characteristics.

Characteristics
This is a happy, active little dog.

Temperament
Although he is playful and outgoing, he should also be gentle, sensitive and affectionate.

Head and skull
The head should be in balance with the overall appearance of the dog. Lengthwise, there should be three parts muzzle to five parts skull. If a line is drawn from the outside corners of the eyes to the nose, it should form the shape of an equilateral triangle. The stop (the indentation between the eyes where the nose bones meet the skull) is slightly accentuated, and the nose is large, prominent and black. Although the Bichon Frisé appears to have a very round head, this has more to do with coat trim than with skeletal conformity—the skull is actually only slightly rounded.

Eyes
The Bichon was bred to be a companion dog, so his looks have been selected to be as appealing as possible. The large, round eyes bring out the nurturing instinct in humans (as they tend to remind us of a baby's features), so it is no surprise that the Bichon is famed for these characteristics. The eyes are dark, look forward, and have an alert expression. They are surrounded by dark "haloes" (round areas of dark-colored skin), which draw further attention to the eyes.

The Bichon is a well-balanced dog with no exaggeration.

Ears

The ears hang close to the head, and are disguised with long flowing hair. Set on slightly higher than eye level, the ears come forward when the dog is alert, framing and accentuating the wonderfully expressive eyes. The ear leathers reach half-way along the muzzle when extended.

Mouth

The jaws are strong, and the dog should have a full set of teeth in a scissor bite (where the top teeth closely overlap the bottom ones). The lips are fine, black and tight (not droopy).

Neck

The neck is long and arched, measuring about one-third the length of the body. It should flow smoothly into the dog's shoulders, and should carry the head high and proud.

Forequarters

The shoulders are the same length as the upper arm, which should be held close to the body. The legs are straight and medium-boned (not too fine).

The pasterns (effectively the dog's "foot"— the area between his "wrist" and the pads/toes) should be short. When viewed from the front, they appear straight, but, from the side, you can see that they slope slightly.

In the US, the dewclaws can be removed, something that UK breeders generally do (although there is no ruling either way in the Breed Standard).

Body

The chest is well developed, allowing free movement of the legs, and the rib cage is well sprung (neither flat nor barrel-shaped). The loin (the dog's "waist") is muscular and there is a slight tuck up.

Hindquarters

The thighs are broad and muscular. The stifles ("knees") are well bent, and the leg from the hock to the footpad is perpendicular.

Feet

The feet should be rather catlike (tight and round) and have black pads.

Tail

The tail is set on level with the dog's back. It curves gently over so that the hair (not the tail itself) lies along the dog's topline.

Gait/movement

A Bichon should move freely and effortlessly, always maintaining a level topline. When moving away from you, the rear footpads should be visible.

Coat

A great deal of information on the coat and on trimming is given in the AKC Standard—probably because presentation is held in far higher esteem in the States than in the UK (remember—it was a grooming makeover that reversed the breed's fortunes—see page 12). In

Judges look for a free-moving gait, where the topline remains level.

fact, the UK Standard states that dogs may be presented untrimmed, although this is very rarely done.

The undercoat is soft and dense; the topcoat is more curly and coarse to the touch. When touched, there should be a "springy" feel to the coat; it should not be flat. Length-wise the coat is about 3–4 inches (7–10 cm), and is trimmed to complement the natural contour of the dog's body.

Color

The coat should be white. In the UK, cream or apricot markings are acceptable only until the age of 18 months.

In the US, buff, cream or apricot markings are permissible on the ears or bodies of puppies; however, in mature dogs, such markings are still acceptable, provided that they constitute 10 percent or less of the entire coat.

Size

The UK Standard gives the ideal height as being 9–11 inches (23–28 cm) to the shoulders. The US Standard states that preference is given to 9.5 to 11.5 inches (24–29 cm). There is some lee-way, although dogs and bitches should not fall outside the range of 9–12 inches (23–30 cm).

REGISTRATION

In most countries, only animals that are registered with the national kennel club are allowed to compete, so your first step should be to make sure that your Bichon has all his papers. If your dog is not registered, and you cannot get him registered (e.g., if one or both of his parents are not pure-bred, registered dogs themselves), this does not necessarily bar him from competing in certain types of shows (see below), but it will prevent him from competing in kennel club–affiliated shows.

GROOMING

It is often said that a slightly less-than-spectacular dog can do very well in the show ring with the right handler and the right grooming. The converse is also true—a "perfect dog" with a shabby coat and poor handling can fail to be placed at all.

Grooming is one of the most important aspects of showing Bichons. Most people severely underestimate the level of work involved in keeping a Bichon's coat in perfect condition. The cost of regular visits to the grooming parlor can be prohibitive, and it is not always practical if you have to travel a few hundred miles to a particular show. Most experienced exhibitors do it themselves, but remember that it takes years to perfect the technique.

If you are starting off, try to enlist the help of someone more experienced for your first year or two of showing. Most Bichon people are very friendly, and with perseverance, you are sure to find some kind soul to help you.

RING-TRAINING

As mentioned above, a dog's success in the show ring is in no small way determined by the handler's ability to show off the dog to his best advantage. The best way to achieve this is to join a ring-training class. These are very similar to the training classes you may have attended with your Bichon as a puppy, but the emphasis is on the skills needed in the show ring rather than on basic obedience.

At a ring-training class, your Bichon will be taught how to stand correctly and how to move so that his gait can be assessed. He will also be taught to become familiar with the judge running his or her hands over the dog's body to assess conformation. An additional benefit is that your Bichon will learn to do what is asked of him while surrounded by other dogs in a highly distracting environment.

Your national kennel club will provide you with contact details of ring-training clubs in your area.

You may need to enlist expert help to present your Bichon for the show ring.

Practice posing your Bichon at home, so he will be relaxed and happy when you show him in the ring.

TIPS FOR SUCCESS

If the high standards covered here have not put you off, and you are still determined to have a go at showing, prepare yourself for an awful lot of fun. Most enthusiasts find that, after the initial nerves have worn off, they can't get enough. Here are some tips to ensure that your show career has the best start possible:

- Start off by visiting shows as a spectator only. Get to know the dogs and speak to their breeders. You'll be amazed at what you learn.
- Join a breed club and attend its seminars. You will learn a lot and can make many useful contacts and friends.
- Go to ring-training classes. Remember that you must not let down your dog with incorrect handling.
- Be aware of the time and money you will need to spend on your dog's appearance, and try to make sure that your own appearance is up to the same standard.
- It takes time, money, patience and hard work to achieve success, but, with the right dog, you will get there if you persevere.
- Most important of all, remember that your Bichon is special. He should be treated as a much-loved pet first and foremost, and as a show dog second. Even if he fails to be placed, he should remain the most special dog in the world to you.

AND THE AWARD FOR . . .

Helen Pugh, from Liverpool, Merseyside, and her Bichon, Oscar (Quissmar the Quiz Master at Verseau), have a very special relationship. Recently, they have taken up showing.

"Oscar is our 'lifesaver dog' and our very first Bichon. He was bought as a family pet at a time when our other dog, a six-month-old Shih Tzu, had just undergone life-saving surgery with only a 30 percent chance of survival. Oscar was the most loving and gentle dog imaginable, and I still believe that, had it not been for Oscar, our little Shih Tzu would not have made it.

"Not long after we got Oscar, the friend who had told us about his litter asked me if she could show him at dog shows. She thought Oscar had real 'sparkle.' At the time, my children were 7 and 10 and quite demanding, so I agreed on the provision that I wouldn't have to get too involved myself. Little did I know!

"I had to take Oscar to ring training classes to prepare him for showing, and it was obvious that he loved it. He picked up all the techniques really quickly. At the tender age of six months and one week he was a star in the making, and it was time for our first show. I was just as excited as he was! Sadly, he didn't get placed, and I must admit that I felt a little jealous about it, but it didn't put us off. Oscar's breeder, Ally Marquiss, suggested that we have another go at a different show and we jumped at the chance.

"The next show we entered was a local Open show, and I was incredibly nervous. I groomed him as best I could, but I was really grateful when Ally came along and took over. Show Bichons have a really precise cut; they look so great in the ring that it's difficult to appreciate the time and effort that goes into preparation until you have to do it yourself.

"The show was a complete disaster. At Oscar's previous show, we were given our ring number at the benches, but at an Open show you are given your number when you enter the ring. When I was given mine, I couldn't get the clip to open, and by the time I had finished struggling with it, everyone else was already lined up in the ring with their dogs neatly stacked. I tried to place Oscar as quickly as possible for the judge to give him the once over, but, by this time, all the other entrants were moving swiftly around the ring, showing off their dogs' gaits. Hastily, I put Oscar on the lead and tried to catch up, but all I succeeded in doing was choking poor old Oscar and he ended up

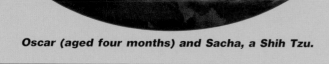

Oscar (aged four months) and Sacha, a Shih Tzu.

Continued overleaf

" I wore the rosette proudly all day, and on the journey home! "

being sick in the ring. A steward ran off to get a mop, and there I was, stood out on my own with treats, a ring number and a choking dog. I could have died of embarrassment! We managed to overcome this and carried on until the end, but needless to say, we finished last.

"Strangely, I somehow found myself entering Oscar for our first Championship show in May 2002. Thinking of our last experience, I was again really nervous, but this time I had learned from my mistakes. We arrived two hours early to make sure we had enough preparation time, and Ally was on hand to help with the grooming. I have to admit that, until then, I didn't really know exactly what I'd let myself in for in deciding to show a Bichon.

"Everything went really smoothly this time, and we were placed second, which qualified us for Crufts. I couldn't believe it! I was absolutely ecstatic and I wore my rosette proudly all day and on the journey home. All my family were really pleased for me. After that, Oscar was placed at most of the shows we entered, although I didn't do them all because of family commitments and the costs involved.

"Our first year in the show world was definitely a learning experience. The most difficult aspect was the grooming. I discovered that, if I was to get anywhere, I desperately needed to get a grip on the grooming, and so I attended a seminar. Then I managed to persuade some unfortunate souls to let me practice the trim on their dogs, and I tried to master the techniques of drying and finishing off. I am very much a novice, and Ally still helps me to groom Oscar just before a

The professional touch: Helen showing Oscar when he qualified for Crufts.

Photo by Alan V Walker

show, but I am slowly getting there. Grooming a Bichon is an art that takes time to master.

"Our second year was when we really started to make progress. Oscar was placed fifth out of a very big class at the UK Toy Dog show. We couldn't have hoped for a better start to the season, and it set the tone for the remainder. He achieved three firsts, one second and two third places. Our crowning moments of 2003 came at Crufts and the Maghull and Merseyside Open respectively. At Crufts, Oscar was placed Reserve in the Special Yearling Dog (a class for dogs under two years old), and at the Open, he was placed Reserve Best in Show and received his first cup! I felt so proud. It had been a fantastic year for both of us, and I no longer felt like the 'new one.'

"I've definitely got the bug now, and I have started campaigning my new Bichon puppy Cora (Dobrugh Dangerous Leaison for Verseau). At her very first show, she achieved Best Puppy, and, at her first Championship show, she was placed second in a variety class—there were no Bichon classes. In March 2004, she entered her first Championship show in Ireland, where she got Best Puppy and Toy Puppy Group 3.

"Despite my protestations about not having the time and not wanting to get too involved, I have been totally sucked into the show world. I have made a great friend in Oscar's breeder, Ally, and I have the chance to get away from work and family commitments and just be me. The grooming side of things allows me to express my artistic side, although I must admit that it just seemed like plain hard work when I first started. After my disastrous Open show when I first started,

Bitten by the showing bug: Helen with Oscar, Cora, and Sacha.

I quickly learned not to take it all too seriously, although there are certainly those who do. For me, it's all about having fun and enjoying myself with my wonderful dog. By far the best bit is seeing Oscar in the ring—he just loves to show!"

BREEDING

When people get involved in the show world, they often become interested in breeding, which can result in their taking up the challenge of trying to breed a litter of typical, healthy Bichon pups, with—who knows—a couple of stars in the making?

The first step is deciding which dog to breed to which bitch. A breeder will have a picture of the ideal Bichon Frisé in mind, thanks to the Breed Standard. It is then a case of choosing a dog that most closely resembles the ideal, who will also be a good match for the bitch. For example, if a bitch is slightly less outgoing than she should be, a breeder would be looking to mate her to a good specimen of the breed that is bold and confident.

Here are two examples of quite different methods of breeding, which have produced equally magnificent results.

Linebreeding

This is where dogs of a similar type are bred together. They are of the same "line" (family) but are not close relations—for example, they might be cousins. The benefit of linebreeding is that a breeder is able to predict the outcome of the mating far more easily. The puppy is likely to have the family characteristics that the breeder has aimed for. However, unlike inbreeding, where immediate family members are mated (such as father to daughter) there are fewer health risks.

Featured: UK. Am. Can. Austrl. Lux. Belg. and Int. Champion Sulyka Hot n' Spicy JW. Champion on three continents, and the first UK-based Bichon to become an International Champion, "Alvin" was bred by Roger and Sue Dunger. His parents, Sulyka Diamonique and Sulyka Bingo, share common—and outstanding—relatives in their pedigrees (Ch. Sulyka Puzzle and Ch. and Austrl Ch. Leijazulip Jazz of Zudiki).

UK Int. Am. Can. Austr. Lux. Belg. Champion Sulyka Hot n' Spicy JW.

Parents	Grandparents	Great-Grandparents	Great-Great-Grandparents
Sulyka Bingo	Ch. Sulyka Puzzle	NZ Ch. Puffin Billy Of Sulyka	UK Ir. Ch. Sulyka Snoopy
			Vythea Fragrance
		Facination Of Zudiki At Sulyka	UK Aust. Ch. Leijazulip Jazz Of Zudiki
			Petite White Velvet
	Sulyka Belinda Bubbles	Honeylyn Sammy Soapsud	Bossy Boots Of Honeylyn
			Honeylyn Silken Tassel Of Sulyka
		Sulyka Sasha Of Honeylyn	NZ Ch. Puffin Billy Of Sulyka
			Sulyka Peppermint Patti
Sulyka Diamonique	Janpal December's Boy Of Honeylyn	Honeylyn Sammy Soapsud	Bossy Boots Of Honeylyn
			Honeylyn Silken Tassel Of Sulyka
		Clanmarret Dream	Shamaney Stepping Out At Kynismar
			Clanmarret Bijou
	Sulyka Pollyanna	Sulyka Garfield	Ch. Sulyka Puzzle
			Snuggle Up To Sulyka
		Facination Of Zudiki At Sulyka	UK Aust. Ch. Leijazulip Jazz Of Zudiki
			Petite White Velvet

Outcrossing

This is a method of breeding where two dogs from entirely different lines are bred together. Breeders generally introduce an outcross mating every now and again, to introduce fresh "blood" so that their lines do not become stale or run the risk of being too closely related to each other. It can help to improve a line too—with a breeder being able to introduce a quality that may be weak in their own line.

Featured: Champion Bylena Tinsletown, who has six Challenge Certificates, four Reserve Challenge Certificates and numerous Best of Breed titles. She received her first RCC at 11 months of age, and was made a Champion when she was just over a year old. The daughter of Hicker Lucy in the Sky, her breeder, Lena Martindale, went to another line, as she thought she was in danger of being too line-bred. After 9 or 10 generations of using dogs in the same line, it was time for new blood. The sire, Ch. Appleacre's Any Dream Will Do J.W., was himself an out-cross.

Ch. Bylena Tinsletown: Outcross breeding.

Parents	Grandparents	Great-Grandparents	Great-Great-Grandparents
Ch. Appleacre's Any Dream Will Do J.W.	Ch. Sargeta's Davilliam Of Bylena	German Ch. Bylena Winner's Boy Of Sargeta	Bylena Winner Take All
			Sargeta's Something Special
		Lasting Fame Of Sargeta	Snarsnoz Domino
			Sargeta's Something Special
	Appleacre's Anagram J.W.	Ch. Sulyka Puzzle	Puffin Billy Of Sulyka
			Facination Of Zudiki At Sulyka
		Appleacre's Amethyst	Appleacre's Milord August J.W.
			Appleacre's Opal Aureole
Hicker Lucy In The Sky To Bylena	Hicker Northern Exposure	Hicker Here Comes The Son	Ch. Hicker Luke Who's Here
			Hicker Lucy Pussy
		Sarabande Maid By Magic For Hicker	Ch. Vythea Jumpin' Jack Flash
			Sarabande Sheer Magic
	Hicker Snow Angel	Honeylyn Sammy Soapsud	Bossy Boots of Honeylyn
			Honeylyn Silken Tassel Of Sulyka
		Hicker Snowsanna	Melsel The Charmer At Hicker
			Hicker Snow White

FROM PUP TO CHAMPION

UK. Int. Lux. & Belg. Ch. Dreamweaver of Sulyka (aka Dee)

Sue and Roger Dunger choose their Bichon puppies at just eight weeks of age. "At this time they are in proportion," says Sue. "After this, they change many times, so we must not be tempted to change our minds. The same proportions will return when the puppies are older."

Here is Dee at eight weeks. She is well balanced, has dark eyes, black pigment, and the thick, soft, curly coat. At this age, small patches of beige on the ears and body are quite acceptable—they soon disappear.

Dee at five months. Pups at this age can appear leggy, but each part of the body grows at a different time and rate, so be patient! Around this time, the Bichon pup often seems to have outgrown his coat, but it will catch up again quite quickly.

At 12 months, the Bichon should be in balance and the puppy coat should be changing to a thick adult coat. The face furnishings grow, so the ears cannot be seen separate from the face coat.

At two years of age, a mature Bichon emerges with a thick coat and black pigment that appears to intensify through the ice-white coat. The body matures to give a well-rounded appearance—and if the coat is cared for correctly, the dog can look like a million dollars!

LANCELOT'S LEGACY

James and Kay Mitchell of the Sasikay Kennels in Fair Oaks, California, have been showing their Bichons for 15 years, and in that time they have founded a dynasty of Champion Bichons.

"In a way, we fell into showing Bichons purely by accident. Our first Bichon, Snuggles, was actually given to my former employer, who wanted a puppy out of her, so we decided to breed her just one time. We kept a puppy from the litter, Sugar, and she was so nice that one of our friends, Virginia Boswell, persuaded us to show her.

"We were incredibly nervous at our first show with Sugar, but she did brilliantly. Despite our inexperience, she took a Group IV (that is, out of all breeds represented in the Non-Sporting Group, Sugar came in fourth). We really enjoyed the whole day. Everyone was very nice to us and we loved seeing all the dogs looking so beautiful.

PROFESSIONAL HANDLER
"We decided to breed Sugar and then began showing one of her sons, Lancelot (Ch. Kay's Excalibur Lancelot, ROM). This time, we employed a professional handler—Paul Flores.

Continued overleaf

Ch. Sasikay Paray Be My Love: One in a long line of home-bred Champions.

"We handle the Bichons ourselves because it is so much fun!"

"Lancelot was a beautiful dog to watch in the show ring, and he never lost a show while Paul was showing him. With Paul's help, it wasn't long before Lancelot became a Champion, and, by that time, we were both hooked on showing.

"We have just finished our 37th Champion. Lancelot is the sire of an additional eight Champions. All the other Champions are descendants of Lancelot. Before they became Champions, several of our dogs took Best of Breed and were placed II, III and IV in the Non-Sporting Group.

HIGH QUALITY

"We begin showing our puppies when they reach six months of age. Now, we tend to handle them ourselves, because it is so much fun. As they get older, we use a professional handler if the dogs haven't finished their Championship requirements. We do this because we need to get the older dogs finished in order to start showing the younger ones.

"We are blessed with high-quality litters, and we have had as many as four show-quality puppies in one litter. All our puppies go to their

Stars of the ring—but the Bichons are also much-loved pets.

Ch. Sasikay Saks Wunderkind (Amadeus).

new homes before being shown because they leave home prior to six months. However, we try to show them at an early age to get their owners enthusiastic about continuing in showing.

"Showing is a great sport for dog owners. Our dogs compete because we want to show our potential breeding stock, so we have a high level of show-quality dogs among our puppies. We would advise anyone thinking of taking up showing to make sure that they acquire a show-quality puppy before beginning. Your dog may seem like the most beautiful creature to you, but it's what the judge thinks in the show ring that counts.

"It's also important to understand just what is involved in presentation. When you're starting out, it helps to have an experienced groomer available—someone who not only knows the correct coat pattern for the Bichon, but who is also available to help get the dog ready for the show ring. If you become serious about showing,

you can learn to do your own grooming, so that you can go to any show without having to depend on anyone else.

COMPETITIVE EDGE

"The only other advice we would offer is to be prepared for the competitiveness that goes on. We have worked very hard with our club members to create an atmosphere where we compete in the show ring but we socialize and have fun together outside the ring. Unfortunately, some people are so competitive that they lose sight of the importance of having friends when you are at a show. Not everyone is like this, but it is something that the novice exhibitor will need to be prepared for.

"We love showing our dogs. It can be very hard work—especially with all the coat care involved—but the joy of seeing a perfectly groomed Bichon moving beautifully in the ring is incomparable."

CHAPTER EIGHT

HEALTH CARE

Health-wise, the Bichon Frisé is remarkably trouble free. There are a few breed-associated problems, but they are largely those that are shared with other popular small breeds.

PREVENTIVE CARE

Most people think that preventive canine care is primarily concerned with vaccination and worming, but other problems have to be addressed. Responsible preventive care involves the following:

- A vaccination program tailored to suit the needs of your dog, your lifestyle and your environment.
- Comprehensive parasite control.
- Adequate exercise, tailored to your dog's age and needs. Bichons are robust, active people dogs, and, if fit, will happily match your pace and endurance.
- Regular grooming.

- Training—Bichons love people and enjoy training. Inquire about puppy socialization and training classes when you make arrangements for vaccination.

Bichons on both sides of the Atlantic have dense undercoats although the standards differ in respect to the fineness of the top coat. Grooming is essential, even for nonshow pets. The coat must receive regular attention to avoid very serious matting.

Grooming involves more than coat attention. Ears, eyes and teeth should all receive regular inspection in order to avoid problems (see Chapter Five).

VACCINATION

Vaccination, or inoculation (throughout this chapter, the terms will be used synonymously) stimulates the dog to produce active immunity against one or more diseases without developing any symptoms of that disease. This is achieved by altering the pathogens (disease causing bacteria or viruses) so that they cannot cause the disease but at the same time ensuring that they still stimulate the body to build up protection (immunity).

The pathogens are killed (inactivated) or weakened (attenuated) to render them safe. Once altered, the appropriate pathogens can be introduced into the body by various routes. For example, vaccination against kennel cough (infectious bronchotracheitis) is by the administration of nasal drops.

Inoculations generally involve injections, popularly referred to as "jabs" or "shots." Irrespective of whether the vaccine is inactivated or attenuated, the body produces an active immunity. This lasts a variable time, depending on factors such as the vaccine, disease, and age and health of the dog.

Puppies acquire immunity from the first milk—colostrum.

Puppy immunity

Puppies are usually born with some immunity that is acquired from their mother while still in the womb. The necessary antibodies are carried in the blood and cross the placenta into the puppy. This is called acquired or passive immunity. It lasts only for about three weeks if not regularly reinforced via antibodies absorbed from the bitch's milk when suckling.

In the first week of life, puppies suckling from the dam receive an extra boost of immunity. This first milk, or colostrum, contains many antibodies that help to protect the pups and reinforce their passive immunity levels.

Passive protection starts to wane once weaning begins. It disappears about a month after the pup has left the mother. This is the danger period for the puppy since he is susceptible to any naturally acquired infection.

One of the aims of vaccine manufacturers is to develop vaccines that will confer solid protection in the shortest possible time, even when circulating maternal antibodies are present.

Canine vaccines are now available that will give protection by 10–12 weeks of age. This affords your puppy early immunity and allows early socialization and training.

Let your new puppy get over the stress of his new surroundings for a day or two and then call your vet. If totally new to pet owning, inquire about vaccinations, but also related matters: costs, appointment details and facilities of the practice (e.g., do they do house calls, have in-house emergency services, etc.). Also ask about puppy classes. These socialization classes are good fun and lay the foundations of training and canine etiquette. They allow controlled interaction between puppies of all ages and breeds.

Boosters

Vaccination does not give lifelong immunity. Reinforcement (boosting) will be required. Most killed vaccines require boosting at least every 12 months. Most canine vaccines are multivalent (i.e., they cover several diseases with one injection). Short-acting (usually inactivated) components are usually also incorporated into the multi-disease protective injection. The time of re-inoculation (boosting) of the product as a whole is based on the component that gives the shortest protection. Although protection against distemper and hepatitis (canine adenovirus—CAV1) will last much longer than a year, when this is combined with leptospirosis, a killed vaccine, the manufacturer's recommendation will be for an annual booster of the combined vaccine.

Vaccination reactions

In response to owners' concerns regarding possible vaccination reactions, it is now advised that primary vaccination and boosters be tailored to individual requirements. This involves assessing the dog's own level of protection against specific diseases (which may require testing), as well as the prevalence of certain diseases within the dog's locality (which can vary significantly between areas). Discuss this with your veterinary surgeon at the time of your puppy's first visit.

Vaccines should be assessed in terms of risks and benefits. My view is that the risk of re-emergence of these killer diseases is very real if we allow our pets' immune status to fall dangerously.

Any dog's resistance to a variety of diseases can be determined from a small blood sample. This will indicate whether boosting is required for any particular disease. The benefit is that unnecessary inoculation is avoided, but the disadvantage is that such a procedure is considerably more expensive than a combined booster injection. The stress to your Bichon should also be considered. A simple jab is much less stressful than taking a blood sample.

If you have concerns, discuss them with your veterinarian; that way, you can reach your own informed decision.

Core vaccines

These protect against diseases that are serious, fatal or difficult to treat. In Britain, these include distemper, parvovirus and hepatitis (adenovirus) disease. In North America, rabies is also included. In the UK, rabies vaccinations are necessary if you intend to travel to any of the countries in the PETS scheme (see panel on page 116). This allows entry or reentry into Britain without having to undergo the mandatory six months' quarantine.

Noncore vaccines

These include inoculations against bordetella (kennel cough) and leptospirosis (kidney disease). In the US, other diseases, such as

Your veterinarian will know about the incidence of disease in your area.

coronovirus (which causes diarrhea) and borellia (Lyme disease—which causes infective polyarthritis) are also included.

Which noncore vaccines are used depends upon a risk assessment in conjunction with your veterinarian.

Vaccine program

Veterinary opinion today is that primary inoculation and the first annual booster (when the pup is about 15 months of age) is sound preventive medicine. These should include both core vaccines and those noncore components considered appropriate. Future vaccinations and their frequency will then depend upon such factors as local infection levels, breed susceptibilities, and lifestyle (e.g., whether you go to shows, training classes, boarding kennels, etc.).

Canine distemper

Canine distemper is no longer widespread in most developed Western countries, solely because of vaccination. Signs (symptoms) include fever, diarrhea and coughing, with discharges from the nose and eyes. With the "hardpad" variant the pads harden. A significant proportion of infected dogs develop nervous signs, including fits, chorea (twitching of muscle groups) and paralysis.

Thanks to vaccination, distemper is quite rare—but do not be misled! The virus is still out there, awaiting its opportunity. This was demonstrated in Finland only a few years ago when a serious epidemic of distemper occurred solely because of falling levels of immunity in the canine population.

Hepatitis

Also known as adenovirus disease (CAV1), hepatitis signs range from the peracute with death to mild cases where the dog only appears to be a bit off-color. In severe cases, there is usually fever, enlargement of all the lymph nodes (glands) and a swollen liver. Sometimes "blue eye" can occur. The eyes look opaque and bluish because of swelling of the cornea (clear part of the eye). The condition usually resolves quickly without problems.

Parvovirus

This virus is very stable and can survive in the environment for a long time. The disease reached epidemic proportions in Europe and North America in the 1980s. Signs include vomiting and blood-stained diarrhea (dysentery). The rapid development of safe, effective vaccines brought the disease under control in the Western world, although it is still a serious killer, rivaling distemper in many countries.

Rabies

Rabies vaccination is compulsory in many countries, including the United States. In Britain, it is mandatory for dogs traveling under the PETS scheme, and for those wishing to enter or reenter Britain. The virus is spread by bites from infected animals. These include foxes in Europe, and skunks, raccoons and stray dogs in America and other parts of the world.

Kennel cough

This syndrome (collection of signs) is considered to be caused by several pathogens, including parainfluenza viruses and bordetella bacteria. In North America, parainfluenza is considered to be the primary cause; in Britain, bacterial bordetella is considered the culprit. Distemper and adenovirus can also play a part.

Irrespective of the cause, the disease is not usually life-threatening, except in very young and very old dogs. A persistent cough for three to four weeks is the main symptom, which results in the rapid spread of the disease. Recently a virulent strain has been discovered, that can cause serious bronchopneumonia.

A parainfluenza component has been incorporated in multivalent vaccines for several years. Manufacturers recommend annual re-vaccination, but in high risk situations (e.g. boarding kennels, shows, etc.), more frequent revaccination is advised.

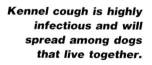

Kennel cough is highly infectious and will spread among dogs that live together.

As well as protecting your dog against potentially fatal diseases, vaccinations are essential if you intend to travel with your Bichon. When planning a trip, plan for your dog as well. Learn all the health rules regarding dogs in force in and to your destination, have your dog vaccinated in advance of your departure and be sure to have that health certificate where you can reach it when requested.

Unlike parainfluenza, bordetella is not incorporated into the usual multivalent vaccines. It is usually administered separately via nasal drops. These have been shown to give better immunity than conventional inoculation by injection. There is also a combined parainfluenza and bordetella intranasal vaccine available.

If you go to shows, training classes or if you regularly board your Bichon, think about regular routine protection against bordetella and parainfluenza—possibly even more frequently than once every year. Your veterinarian will advise.

Leptospirosis

Leptospirosis is caused by bacteria and not viruses. Protection against two diseases is currently provided by the killed (inactivated) leptospirosis vaccine.

Leptospira canicola is spread mainly in the urine of infected dogs. *Leptospira icterohaemorrhagiae* is spread by rats. Both types cause disease in dogs and are zoonotic (meaning they can spread between species, including humans).

The leptospirosis vaccine is probably one of the shortest acting of all the various components in multivalent vaccines.

Canine coronavirus

This virus can cause diarrhea, particularly in puppies. The disease is usually mild and responds to supportive therapy. A vaccine is available in North America and some European countries, but not currently in Britain.

Canine herpes virus

Fading puppy syndrome has many causes, but it has recently been found that one of the major causes of puppies dying in the womb (resulting in reduced litter size) or shortly after birth is canine herpes virus (CHV). A vaccine is now available, which is unique in that it is given to infected bitches. One injection is given at mating and another before whelping. The vaccine has been shown to significantly reduce the problem of fading puppies in some cases. Immunity is short, however. The course has to be repeated with each litter.

Lyme disease

This disease, caused by bacteria (spirochaetes), is carried by ticks whose bite can transmit the disease to dogs and humans. It is common in parts of North America and also occurs in Britain. It causes acute polyarthritis in both dogs and people. Fever, heart, kidney and neurological problems can also occur. Although vaccines are available in North America, there is currently no licensed vaccine available in Britain.

PARASITES

Parasite control is an important part of preventive health care and is essential for all dogs—irrespective of size or lifestyle. Parasites can be divided into two groups:

- Ectoparasites live on the surface of the host, and include fleas, lice, ticks and mites.
- Endoparasites live within the host. Worms are the most well known, although there are other important endoparasites.

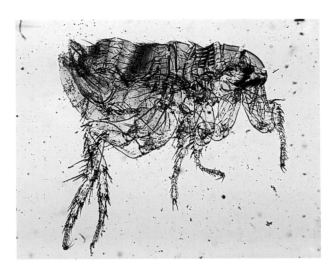

The dog flea—Ctenocephalides canis.

ECTOPARASITES

Fleas

In my experience, Bichons are not usually seriously troubled with fleas but they are the most common ectoparasites found on dogs. Therefore, routine flea control is important. Fleas can be picked up from the environment or from contact with other animals.

Some dogs will carry a very high flea burden without problem, whereas others will show evidence of typical flea allergy dermatitis (FAD) even though no fleas are visible on the dog. This is the situation I have found most commonly with the Bichon. Often, a pet cat is the culprit. Once hypersensitivity (allergy) occurs, a bite from one flea is sufficient to start serious pruritis (itching). Even if no fleas can be found on the Bichon, there is usually evidence of flea dirts (small black specks). Always check for these when grooming.

Fleas are not host-specific. Cat and hedgehog fleas can affect a range of other animals, including ourselves and our dogs.

The life cycle

Effective control involves both adult fleas on the animals and also the immature stages, which develop in the home. Fleas need a meal of blood to complete their life cycle. The female flea then lays eggs (usually on the dog, although they can lay them in the environment if the temperature and humidity are right). Eggs laid on the dog soon drop to the ground. Under suitable conditions, they develop into immature forms (larvae) in carpets or gaps between floorboards or sometimes outside. Many pet dogs and cats have areas—even in tiny town gardens—where they like to lie. Such areas can be difficult to render flea-free!

Under ideal conditions, the life cycle can be completed in only three weeks. Sometimes fleas can live without feeding for more than a year. This is why dogs and people can be bitten when entering a property that has been left unoccupied for some time.

Control methods

Adult fleas account for only approximately 5 percent of the total flea population. Control of the other 95 percent, consisting of immature stages, is more difficult. Few environmental insecticides have any effect against immature fleas, so an insecticide with prolonged action should be used. This will be effective against any subsequently emerging adults. Control in the home should also involve thorough vacuuming to remove any flea larvae.

Oral preparations are available, which prevent the completion of the flea life cycle. The compound is transferred to the adult flea when it bites the dog for the all-essential blood meal.

There are many effective preparations to control adult fleas on the dog. Sprays can be used, but most dogs dislike the noise, and care must be taken to avoid the eyes. Powders are effective but messy, particularly in the long coat of the Bichon. Insecticidal baths are useful for killing adult fleas in the coat, but they do not have a prolonged effect. Bathing should always be combined with other methods of flea control to prevent rapid reinfestation.

Prolonged-action spot-on preparations are very effective and are easy to apply. They contain chemicals that are lethal to the flea. These are dissolved in a substance that spreads through the invisible fat layer on the skin. When the flea bites your pet for that all-essential blood meal, it has to penetrate the fat layer to get to the blood supply, and, by so doing, ingests the ectoparasiticide.

Within 24 hours of application, your dog has total protection against fleas for approximately two months. The preparation remains effective even if the dog gets wet or is bathed (provided it is not more than once or twice between applications). It is important to reapply the preparation according to the manufacturer's recommendations. This is usually every 30 or 60 days, depending on the product. Some preparations are also effective against certain

Spot-on flea treatment is effective and easy to apply.

endoparasites, particularly roundworms. These are called endectocides.

Lice

Lice are rarely a problem in this breed. They require direct contact for transmission and, unlike fleas, the whole life cycle occurs on the host. The eggs (nits) are attached to individual hairs. Infestation is usually associated with violent irritation and often affects the head and ears. Unlike fleas, lice can be controlled by bathing the dog in an effective ectoparasite shampoo.

Ticks

Ticks are carriers of various diseases. Lyme disease (borelliosis), babesiosis and ehrlichiosis are examples. Although these diseases have been recognized in the UK, they are more common in warmer parts of Europe and the United States. Several flea and lice preparations are effective for tick control, and some are licensed for use on ticks. Follow your vet's advice.

Cheyletiellosis

Cheyletiella yasguri, the causal mite, can just be seen by the naked eye as a tiny white speck, hence this condition's other name—"walking dandruff." This is not usually a problem in Bichons Frisés, but the mite is zoonotic and can cause intense irritation, particularly in children. Adult dogs, often showing no signs, act as carriers in kennels. Sprays, bathing and spot-on preparations are all effective. Other pets should be treated to ensure that reinfestation does not recur. Veterinary advice should be sought.

Harvest mites

These are the larvae (immature forms) of a mite that lives in decaying organic matter. They are red in color and are just visible to the naked eye. Bichons, particularly if exercised in fields and woodlands with a chalky soil, can become infested. Feet, muzzle and head are target areas, and intense irritation results.

Any of the usual insecticidal sprays or washes are effective, but reapplication is necessary if you live in an area where this larval mite is rife.

Mange

Mange is a parasitic skin disease caused by microscopic mites. Three types can occur in the Bichon.

❶ **Demodectic mange:** Demodex mites live in the hair follicles and sebaceous glands of many normal dogs. They cause problems only if the dog is immuno-incompetent when the mite starts to multiply. Therefore, the condition is not as contagious as the other types of mange. In multi-dog households, often only one pet will be affected. Signs include inflammation and hair loss. Itching is often minimal but secondary bacterial infection can be a problem. Veterinary treatment, using modern preparations, is effective once a positive diagnosis has been made, but because of the possible underlying immune problem, affected dogs should not be bred.

❷ **Otodectic mange:** Ear mite infestation (otocariasis) is not that uncommon in Bichons, particularly if the home is shared with a cat. Adult cats often carry large numbers of the causal mites, *Otodectes cyanotis*, without symptoms. The signs include head shaking and scratching, and often a brown smelly discharge from the ear. Consult your veterinarian for treatment, which must include in-contact animals.

❸ **Sarcoptic mange (scabies):** This affects many animals, including humans. Children are particularly susceptible and can develop intensely itchy areas on the arms and abdomen as a result of nursing the affected animal. Modern veterinary treatments are effective, but depend on an accurate diagnosis, which sometimes requires repeated skin scrapings. Consult your veterinarian.

ENDOPARASITES

Intestinal worms are by far the most important endoparasites of the dog. Protozoan parasites, such as *Coccidia* and *Giardia*, may also be a problem in certain areas, together with blood-borne parasites, such as *Babesia* and *Ehrlichia*, which occur in the United States and in dogs imported to Britain from areas where the diseases are rife (e.g., southern Europe).

Roundworms

Until relatively recently, puppies were always thought of as being wormy. The development of effective roundworm remedies, and the understanding of the complex life cycle, has now resulted in dramatic reduction of the problem.

The most common roundworm is *Toxocara canis*. This is a large, round, white worm 3–6 inches (7–15 cm), with a complex life cycle. Puppies can be born with toxocariasis acquired from their mother before birth, so worming is essential.

Roundworm larvae can remain dormant in the tissues of adult dogs indefinitely. Under the influence of hormones during pregnancy, they become activated and enter the puppy via the blood. They finally develop into adult worms in the small intestine so the puppy can shed infective eggs only two weeks after birth. Larvae are also passed from the bitch to the puppy during suckling.

A worming program is essential when rearing puppies.

There are now many safe and effective worm treatments available. Endectocides are spot-on preparations similar to those used for flea control. They contain drugs (e.g., selamectin) that are effective against roundworms, heartworms and fleas. Endectocides can be useful if you have difficulty administering oral preparations to your Bichon.

Some preparations are licensed for use in puppies from 14 days of age. Some are available over-the-counter, but veterinary help is worthwhile to establish an effective, lifelong worming strategy.

Tapeworms

Tapeworms are the other common intestinal worms found in the dog. Unlike roundworms they do not have a direct life cycle, so spread is not from dog to dog but has to be through an intermediate host. This varies according to the type of tapeworm, and includes fleas, sheep, horses, rodents and sometimes even humans!

In the dog, the most common type of tapeworm is *Dipylidium caninum*. This worm, which can be up to 20 inches (50 cm), uses the flea as the intermediate host. The worms live in the intestine. Eggs contained within mature segments are shed from the end of the worm and pass out in the dog's feces. These segments are sticky and look like small grains of rice. In infested dogs, they can often be seen around the anus. The segments finally fall to the ground, dry and burst, releasing the microscopic eggs.

Free-living flea larvae eat the fertilized eggs, which develop as the flea matures. When the adult flea is swallowed by a dog, the life cycle of the tapeworm is completed.

Effective treatment involves the tapeworm and eradication of fleas in the environment. Enlist the help of your veterinarian.

Echinococcus species

These are important because of their zoonotic potential. *Echinococcus multilocularis* can cause serious cysts in the lungs of people. Under the PETS scheme, dogs and cats have to be treated with specific remedies against this worm (and so certified) before entry or re-entry to the UK is allowed.

Heartworm

Dirofilaria immitis causes major problems in many of the warmer parts of the world, including North America. Selamectin (mentioned previously) is one of the effective drugs available. Consult your veterinarian if heartworm is a problem in your area.

Other intestinal worms

Hookworms (*Uncinaria* and *Ancylostoma* species), together with whipworms (*Trichuris vulpis*), are occasionally the cause of lack of condition. More severe signs, such as anemia or dysentery, can occur. They are often discovered during routine fecal investigation rather than because the dog is sick. Treatment is uncomplicated with modern preparations from your veterinarian.

Protozoan parasites

Giardia and *coccidia* are gut parasites that can cause diarrhea problems, particularly in puppies. **Giardia** is a water-borne disease, more common in North America than in the UK, although the disease can occur in the UK in imported dogs.

Giardiasis is considered to be zoonotic and is the most common intestinal parasite in humans in America. Nevertheless, there is no conclusive evidence that cysts shed by dogs (and cats) are infective to humans.

Certain blood-borne protozoan parasites, such as *Babesia* and *Leishmania*, are important in southern parts of America and Europe, but at present do not regularly occur in Britain. *Leishmania*, spread by sandflies, constitutes a public health risk.

Bichons are lively dogs, and can get into scrapes.

EMERGENCY CARE AND FIRST AID

The Bichon is a lively little dog and unfortunately emergencies do happen! A basic knowledge of canine first aid never comes amiss, since Bichons can get themselves into all sorts of emergency situations.

First aid is the initial treatment given in any emergency. The purpose is to preserve life, reduce pain and discomfort, minimize the risk of permanent disability or disfigurement, and to prevent further injury.

PRIORITIES

- Keep as calm as possible and try not to panic.
- If possible, get help.
- Contact your own veterinary surgeon (or a local practice if away from home), explain the situation, and ask for help.
- If there is the possibility of internal injury, try to keep your dog as still as possible. With a Bichon, this is easier than with some of the larger breeds.
- If the dog is in shock (see below) warmth is essential. A cardboard box will keep him warm, confined and reasonably still, and is useful for transportation. Use blankets if available, or wrap your Bichon in a coat or even newspaper. Take care that he does not jump out if he suddenly becomes conscious.

• Take your dog to the veterinarian as soon as practicable. Drive carefully, observe the speed limits and, if possible, take someone with you to keep an eye on the dog while you drive, or vice versa.

A, B, C OF FIRST AID

A is for airway

Bichons are lively dogs and love playing with sticks. Do not encourage it. Injuries to the mouth or throat can happen very quickly and result in airway problems, vomiting, collapse or choking, which can obstruct breathing.

• Do your best to clear the mouth and throat to allow the passage of as much air (oxygen) to the lungs as possible.

• Avoid using your bare hands to clear the throat. Your Bichon will be just as panic-stricken as you are, and, if fighting for his life, may well bite in panic.

• Use any blunt object (such as a piece of wood or the back of a spoon) to try to open the mouth. Sometimes you can drop a loop (e.g., a tie or a piece of string) around the upper and lower fang teeth and gently open the mouth.

• Then you can use either a well-gloved hand or a stick wrapped in a cloth to try to clear the throat.

B is for breathing

Check that there are no obvious chest injuries. If there are and the dog appears to be unconscious, you can try mouth-to-nose resuscitation (see below). If the chest appears uninjured but your Bichon is not breathing, do the following:

• Place him on his right side, with both forelegs pulled forward.

• Gently squeeze the chest just behind the elbows, at the same time trying to detect a heartbeat.

• If none can be detected, go on swiftly to cardiac massage (see below).

C is for cardiac function

Despite the Bichon's abundant coat, the heart beat (cardiac pulse) can easily be felt in a healthy dog. Place a hand around the ribs, just behind the elbows. If nothing can be felt and there are no chest injuries, try cardiac massage—cardio pulmonary resuscitation (CPR). This can be successful in starting the heart to beat.

• If your dog is unconscious and you cannot detect a heartbeat, try gently squeezing the ribs in the area, approximately every two seconds.

• Check if you can feel any movement below your fingers every two to three minutes. If there is no sign, continue squeezing.

• If there is no result after five to six minutes, move to mouth-to-nose resuscitation (below).

• Do not attempt CPR if there is a risk of chest injury. Go to mouth-to-nose resuscitation.

If the dog is collapsed but breathing, try to get him to the veterinarian as soon as possible. Otherwise, continue CPR for at least 10 minutes on-site. If there is no result after a few minutes, try mouth-to-nose resuscitation:

- Pull the tongue forward and place a handkerchief over the mouth and nose.
- Hold the mouth shut, and blow gently down the nostrils and mouth.
- If there is no obvious chest injury, also continue CPR.

Check the color of the mucous membranes of the gums or inside the lips. If the dog is bleeding and shocked, the mucous membranes will be pale or white. If bleeding is visible (i.e., external), try to stop it. Treat for shock (see below).

SHOCK

What is shock?

Shock is a complex condition that disrupts the delicate fluid balance of the body. It is always accompanied by a serious fall in blood pressure. Causes include serious hemorrhage, heart failure, heatstroke, and acute allergic reactions (e.g., bee stings).

Signs of shock include the following:
- Rapid breathing
- Rapid heart rate
- Pale mucous membranes
- Severe depression
- A cold feel to the limbs, ears, and other extremities
- Vomiting.

The most important first-aid treatment for shock is to maintain body heat. Avoid external heat, and instead wrap your dog in a blanket or towel and get him to your veterinarian quickly.

The responsible Bichon owner should have a knowledge of first aid.

COMMON FIRST-AID PROBLEMS

Bleeding

Torn nails happen often with Bichons. They are painful and can result in copious bleeding. Any hemorrhage from the limbs should be bandaged fairly tightly, using any clean material.

Bleeding from other parts of the body (e.g., head, ears, etc.) that cannot be bandaged should be controlled by applying a cold-water swab and finger or hand pressure. Seek veterinary help.

Burns and scalds
- Cool the burned or scalded area with cold water as quickly as possible.
- If the affected area is extensive, wrap the Bichon in wet towels.
- If the injury is caused by a caustic substance (such as drain cleaner or bleach), wash with plenty of cold water.
- If the injurty is in the mouth, press a cloth soaked in clean cold water between the jaws.
- Seek professional advice without delay.

Eye injuries
Scratches from bushes and cats' claws are not uncommon injuries. Cold water, or better still, saline solution (contact lens solutions) liberally applied with a pad should be used to cleanse the eye. If the eyeball appears to be injured or if there is any bleeding, try to cover the eye with a pad soaked in cold water and get to your veterinarian as soon as possible.

Fits and seizures
Bichons are not generally predisposed to convulsions (fits) or seizures, but they can occur after a head injury. During a fit, your Bichon is unconscious, but the event is nevertheless pretty terrifying for onlookers.
- If possible, place him in a dark, confined area where he cannot damage himself. A cardboard packing case makes an ideal environment for a dog of this size.
- Touch him as little as possible.
- Most seizures only last a few seconds or minutes at most. It is better to wait until there has been some recovery before going to see the veterinarian.
- If the seizure continues for more than three or four minutes, contact your veterinarian immediately.

Heatstroke
In warm, humid weather, heatstroke (hyper-thermia) can strike rapidly. Inadequately ventilated cars are the main cause of this distressing and frequently fatal condition. However, in warm, humid weather, ill-ventilated rooms are just as dangerous for a dog with a thick coat. Heatstroke can occur without the dog being in direct sunlight. The body temperature rises rapidly and this can result in irreversible damage.

Heatstroke can have devastating effects—in a very short space of time.

First signs are excessive panting, with obvious breathing distress (stertor). Coma and death can quickly follow because of irreversible changes in the blood vessels. Reduce the temperature as quickly as possible. Plunge or bathe the dog in cold water. Place ice on the gums, under the tail and in the groin. Then take the still-wet animal to the veterinarian as soon as possible.

BREED-ASSOCIATED PROBLEMS

Cataracts

A cataract is an opacity in the lens of the eye. Primary cataract occurs in the absence of any other ocular disease. It can affect both eyes and is hereditary. Unlike some breeds, such as the Miniature Schnauzer, in which cataracts can be present from birth (congenital), in the Bichon Frisé and many other breeds, the condition develops when the dog is mature. It is called mature onset hereditary cataract, and is first noticed as a milky appearance of the pupil on the affected side. If you are concerned, consult your veterinary surgeon. Cataract surgery is available and usually carries a good prognosis.

Dental problems

Although tartar build-up and gum disease does occur in the breed, the frequency is minimal compared with some other small dogs. Nevertheless, starting home dental care when your Bichon is first acquired is a useful prophylactic measure (see Chapter Five). If your dog develops bad breath, consult your vet.

Hip problems

Legge Perthes disease, or, to use its more descriptive name, vascular necrosis of the femoral head, is a crippling disease in young, small breeds of dog. It can occur in Bichons Frisés between 4 and 6 months of age, when the puppy becomes lame on one or both hind legs. Cases have also been reported between 9 and 12 months—up to the age when growth plates are absorbed. There is increasing pain and restriction of movement. The condition is known to be hereditary, so affected individuals should not be bred.

The condition is caused by a reduction to the blood supply to the maturing femoral head in the hip joint. Part of the bone dies because of the lack of blood supply, and the joint becomes progressively distorted. This results in pain and ultimately in total disuse of the leg. Treatment, which involves removal of all the diseased bone, is usually very successful.

Slipping kneecaps

This condition is also known as luxating patellae. The patella—or kneecap—slides in a groove at the bottom of the femur (thigh bone). A common congenital problem in small breeds is a shallow groove. This results in the patella slipping out of the groove to the inside of the knee. This is noticed as an intermittent lameness in the young Bichon, often less than six months old. The limb will usually be carried for a number of strides and then the patella relocates spontaneously, resolving the problem. Sometimes, by gently flexing and extending the leg, the

With good care and management, your Bichon should live a long life, free from major health problems.

kneecap can be felt to slip in and out of its groove.

Surgery is extremely successful in the majority of cases. If you are worried that your young Bichon is occasionally lame, consult your veterinary surgeon without delay.

Urolithiasis

This refers to stones anywhere in the urinary tract. In male Bichons, together with other small breeds, the stones tend to cause blockage in the urethra (the tube from the bladder to the exterior). Stones are usually found to be calcium oxalate. Symptoms are straining, and pain when trying to urinate, often with blood. It is important to seek veterinary attention without delay.

SUMMARY

Overall, it is my view that the Bichon suffers with minimal breed-related problems compared with other small breeds. This is a robust, healthy little dog, but, if you ever have any concerns, you should seek veterinary advice at once.